THE GARCIA BOY  A MEMOIR

Published by Big Shoulders Books
DePaul University
Chicago, Illinois

ISBN: 978-0-578-41221-4
Library of Congress Control Number: 2018964141

Photographs: inside front cover by Paul D'Amato; inside back cover by Nick Ulivieri
Big Shoulders Books logo design by Robert Soltys

RAFAEL TORCH

a memoir

foreword by Achy Obejas
afterword by Emily Olson-Torch
edited by Miles Harvey

2019

ABOUT BIG SHOULDERS BOOKS

Big Shoulders Books aims to produce books that engage intimately with the Chicago community and, in the process, give graduate and undergraduate creative-writing students at DePaul University hands-on, practical experience in book publishing. The goal of Big Shoulders Books is to disseminate, free of charge, quality anthologies of writing by and about Chicagoans whose voices might not otherwise be shared. Big Shoulders Books hopes to make small but meaningful contributions to discussions of injustice and inequality in Chicago, as well as to celebrate the tremendous resilience and creativity found in all areas of the city.

The views and opinions expressed in this book do not necessarily reflect those of DePaul University or the College of Liberal Arts and Social Sciences, and should not be considered an endorsement by DePaul for any purpose.

ABOUT OUR FUNDERS

The Garcia Boy: A Memoir was made possible by a grant from the William and Irene Beck Charitable Trust.

Miles Harvey
Editor

Kaitlin Lounsberry and Brittany Schmitt
Managing Editors

Travis Murphy and Matthew J. Postlewaite
Associate Managing Editors

Editorial Staff
Elizabeth Bradley
Nicole Carullo
Samantha Chmara
Andrew Dunaway
Emma Littel-Jensen
Laura Niebrugge
Norah O'Malley
Carlee Post
Theresa Romano
Nadine Worley

INTRODUCTION

by MILES HARVEY

The author of this book is not famous. Even among his fellow writers, few will recognize the name Rafael Torch. I would never have heard of him myself, in fact, if not for a small act of kindness. In 2013, during a literary festival at Southern Illinois University, a man took me aside and offered me a gift.

That man, Jon Tribble, was managing editor of the literary magazine *Crab Orchard Review*, a copy of which he placed in my hands. On page 212, he'd stuck a Post-it note. Opening to the marked section, I found an essay titled "La Villita" by a writer whose name didn't ring a bell.

"I think you should read this," Jon said.

As my eyes fell upon the words "gunned down on a dark street" in the first sentence, I understood why Jon thought I might be interested in the piece. The talk I had given at the festival that day was on *How Long Will I Cry?: Voices of Youth Violence*, a collection of oral histories about the emotional devastation of street violence in Chicago. During 2011 and 2012, while more than 900 people were being murdered all over the city, my creative-writing students at DePaul University and I interviewed people whose lives had been forever changed by the carnage. And while I was very proud of the work we did, the process had left me drained. After years of dealing with stories of loss and pain and horror, I wasn't sure I was ready for another one.

Perhaps sensing my hesitation, Jon looked me straight in the eye.

"I *really* think," he said again, "you should read this."

Because I have a lot of respect for Jon and because he seemed so adamant, I cracked open that copy of *Crab Orchard Review* when I got back home and began to read—skeptically at first, but then, after a paragraph or two, with growing excitement. The essay described the murder of a promising student at a largely Mexican-American high school on the Southwest Side of Chicago and the effect that killing had on his fellow students and his teachers, one of whom was the author. It was a gripping story, but what impressed me most was its knife-sharp prose and epic scope. "La Villita" wasn't just about one tragedy in a lone neighborhood. Its author was attempting to map out not only the physical, cultural and political borders that feed gang rivalries in our cities and ethnic hatreds across the country, but also the psychological borders that can keep daughters and sons of impoverished immigrants from ever attempting to achieve the American Dream. By the time I finished the essay, I was experiencing that high-voltage shudder that shoots through me whenever I encounter a writer with a unique and powerful voice.

I was amazed that I knew nothing about Rafael Torch, and soon I found out why. Two years earlier, he had died of a rare form of cancer, having published only a few essays during his

36 years of life. One of his obituaries also mentioned that he'd left behind an unpublished memoir—a detail that didn't mean much to me at first. But as the years wore on, and as I read "La Villita" over and over again with my students, it began to gnaw at me that a writer I so admired—a writer who had so much to say about my city and my country—might be known to only a handful of enthusiastic readers.

After digging around, I discovered that a copy of the memoir was on file at the University of Chicago, where Torch had earned a master's degree in 2005. So one day I went to Hyde Park to read it. As an experienced editor, I recognized flaws with the draft, especially in terms of structure, but it was equally obvious that the prose was stunning and the material was rich. I decided to approach Emily Olson-Torch, the author's widow, with an idea: What if my creative-writing students and I edited the memoir and released it through Big Shoulders Books, a nonprofit publishing entity at DePaul? I was completely prepared for her to decline the offer, which, after all, involved no money whatsoever. But to my delight, Emily ended up embracing the concept. And thus, this edition of *The Garcia Boy* was born.

Big Shoulders Books is designed to give graduate and undergraduate students at DePaul hands-on, practical experience in book publishing. And for those who worked on *The Garcia Boy*, this extraordinary text proved to be both a one-of-a-kind learning opportunity and an immensely demanding challenge.

Torch, it turned out, had kept revising the book right up until his death, adding and subtracting large sections of material and constantly rethinking and reworking the overall structure. Emily informed us that he never felt he had found exactly the right form for *The Garcia Boy*. As a result, we began the editing process with three markedly different drafts—one of them 200 pages, one 400 pages and one 450 pages. In addition to that, there was also a variety of other writings that Emily had made available to us—outtakes from the book, letters to prospective publishers and agents, blog posts and essays, including the original version of "La Villita."

I asked the students to read and make notes on all these materials, then come up with detailed proposals about how we might move forward. And because I wanted them to always remember the significance of our work, the immense responsibility of being entrusted with a gifted writer's most important project, I also requested that they address their proposals to Torch, in the form of a letter from editor to author. I knew I was asking a lot of them in terms of time commitment and emotional engagement, but they proved more than equal to the task. It turned out that Torch's prose was all the inspiration they needed. Several members of this talented group, in fact, have continued to work on the book long after the class came to an end.

Emily was also a marvelous collaborator, working closely with the students and me throughout the editorial process. She turned out to have great narrative instincts, which proved to be instrumental in helping us shape the book. Our biggest job was one of focus. In various drafts, Torch had attempted to tie his experiences to the sweep of American history, making *The Garcia Boy* a multi-generational tale, starting with his maternal great-grandfather's emigration from Italy in the early years of the 20th century. We decided, however, to structure the book around the author's own life story. And in order to finish that narrative, we added an epilogue—an essay he wrote near the end of his life, as he was both awaiting the birth of his son and battling the cancer that would overtake him less than four months after that child was born.

The title of this book refers to three separate Garcia boys. The first is the author's father, Rafael Garcia, who arrived in the United States in 1972 as an undocumented Mexican immigrant. The second is Sergio Garcia, the 17-year-old student whose killing Torch described in "La Villita." The third, of course, is the author himself. Throughout the book, he juxtaposes his own experiences with those of the other two Garcia boys—the largely absent father who failed to save the author from alcoholism and substance abuse, and the murdered son-figure whom the author failed to save from a tragic life and death on the streets.

Torch also meditates on the struggles of other students at Cristo Rey Jesuit High School, a college-prep academy for Latina and Latino students, many of whom are the daughters and sons of immigrants. Having grown up in the Pilsen and Little Village neighborhoods—the traditional heart of Chicago's Mexican-American community—these young people are often caught between two cultures. The author, meanwhile, is in an inverse predicament. Unable to speak Spanish due to a suburban upbringing in Ohio with his Italian-American mother, he finds himself teaching in the neighborhood where he lived as an infant before his parents' divorce. Being an outsider to the community forces him to confront his own fractured sense of self, a wrenching journey—emotional, intellectual and physical—that drives the narrative of *The Garcia Boy*.

What does it mean to be an American? And how does a person gain (or fail to gain) that identity? Although Torch wrote the book 15 years ago, the questions he poses are more important than ever. Indeed, publication of *The Garcia Boy* comes at a time of national soul-searching over issues of immigration, a time of travel bans and border walls and forced separations of families attempting to enter the country. To the demagogues behind such efforts, "American" means white, English-speaking and Christian, but Torch reminds readers that "the American narrative is never composed of just one story, memory or history." What interests him is exploring "the ways in which we, as Americans, tell stories and the ways we begin to learn about our identities through the act of storytelling."

But as he makes clear from the start, he's also fascinated by how often those narratives are built upon myths, self-deceptions and outright lies. "My father likes to tell stories, and they may not always be true," he asserts in the opening line of the book. Torch's exploration of this impulse to fabricate makes *The Garcia Boy* especially prescient in an age of "alternative facts," when Americans increasingly believe ideas they wish to be true rather than those that are based on actual evidence. But Torch doesn't just describe the "reckless" narratives of his father; he also freely concedes his own tendency to self-mythologize. And for anyone attempting to make sense of his work, this presents real challenges.

Even in what some experts have labeled the "post-truth" era, readers expect a memoir to describe actual events. So in editing *The Garcia Boy*, we have fact-checked the text to the best of our ability and have otherwise endeavored to make clear that certain scenes are products of the author's imagination. Nonetheless, I suspect that Rafael Torch wanted readers to be slightly unsure of where they stand in relation to the narrative, placing them in the same uncomfortable position he often found himself in when listening to his father's marvelous stories about becoming an American. If I'm right about this, his goal was to make us consider how we constantly reinvent our own sense of the past in order to construct identity in the ever-changing present, both in the global village and in La Villita.

But, of course, I can't be sure that my interpretation is correct. As with so many aspects of this project, I wish it were possible to discuss the book and its many nuanced meanings with the author himself.

Never having met Rafael Torch, I have often questioned whether I had the proper insight to edit this book. One thing I am confident about, however, is that the endeavor has always been driven by respect for a fellow writer and by despair at the idea that his work might be lost to obscurity. For me and my students, *The Garcia Boy* has been a labor of love. We offer it to you now in the same spirit it came to me—as a gift.

—*October 1, 2018*

FOREWORD

by ACHY OBEJAS

In the early aughts, I was lucky enough to be teaching creative writing at the University of Chicago, where the students were smart and eager and there wasn't enough homework I could lob at them. This was back before the university had a formal creative-writing program, back when we were just planting the seeds for it, and so there were few classes and students who'd suddenly become addicted to storytelling kept taking the same courses over and over. What this meant was that my classes—small, capped at 12 students—were filled with kids who'd developed an affinity for each other over time. They were a team, cohesive, confederated.

That's what Rafael Torch walked into when I met him: a gathering of 11 students, all white, all from relative privilege, all close and all extremely committed to the word. I can see his slow smile as he scanned the classroom. Rafa didn't look like them; soft-spoken, he didn't really sound like them; a little older than most of them and already scar-bearing, his life was worlds away from most of theirs.

One of the rules—or maybe lack of rules—in my classes was that there was no page limit to submissions. Most creative-writing workshops impose some kind of maximum, usually 15 pages or so of writing, for work to be discussed in class. But this kind of arbitrary page count frequently means we don't get full stories, or we get stories that are crammed into 15 pages when what they need is to breathe, or we get stories that should end at six pages but that their authors feel compelled to elongate.

"Really? No page count?" Rafa asked.

"Really," I said, maybe even a little smugly. The class nodded in unison.

The next day, we all woke up to Rafa's email submission: *The Garcia Boy*, a whopping 330 pages.

Later, much later, when we were laughing about this outlandish move of his, I said, "You just did that *pa' joder.*"

And he blanched. He hadn't heard the expression, he didn't know what I meant. It threw him into a crisis that lasted days. Our e-mails could fill a book, back and forth with the story of why he didn't speak Spanish and why I did and why both were okay, back and forth with what it meant to look like he did and the way people confused him for so many different ethnicities and why people read me as white most times, back and forth with why he didn't always feel entitled to his story and why I insisted he most definitely was.

In class, we tackled Rafa's monster manuscript. Surgically. With sweep. With care. Those white kids weren't afraid to ask the hard questions. After class, he and I would sometimes hang out. He didn't drink, so bars were out and sometimes he'd just come over. He'd borrow armloads of books at a time (he read as if his life depended on it). Sometimes we'd sit in my car for hours, even in the freezing cold.

This is what we did: We talked endlessly. He was hungry, hungry to write and to know how to write, hungry to read books by people he'd never heard of, by other Garcia boys, hungry to be accepted, ravenous, really, for connection. One time, just as the December holiday break had begun, his flight home to his mother's was delayed at O'Hare and he called and asked if I'd come and just hang with him. And I did. We sat there, doodling on the frozen windowpanes, walking around the airport in the wee hours when everything was closed and gated. He finally boarded as the sun was trying to break out of the morning mist.

After Rafa left the University of Chicago, we had less contact. His life was in turmoil. So was mine. He got sick. He got better. At some point, we both decided we wanted to spend time together again around writing. Some former class-mates had put together a post-graduate workshop and invited me and two other professional writers, Bayo Ojikutu and Kalisha Buckhanon, both South Side-based African-American writers of certain repute, to join them. I invited Rafa. He threw *The Garcia Boy* on us again, this time around 250 pages. We were about halfway through it when he dropped out—one of the other writers had come at him rather aggressively about the way he depicted addiction (she would later apologize, acknowledging she was high as a kite when she kicked off the argument)—and he wasn't going to change it but didn't want to make her feel uncomfortable. I begged him to stick it out, but I also realized he was so sick, so weary by then, that this was probably just his way of dropping out without having to talk about the real reasons why.

Plus, by this time he'd fallen in love with Emily and the truth was—he'd eventually confess—he wanted to spend every minute he had with her. He wanted to write. He wanted to consider his life. He only had so much time.

I've often wondered what Rafa—handsome, smart, considerate, uncannily sensitive—would have become had he managed to stay in this world. Of course he would have continued writing. And he would have loved Emily all of his days, and been ever present for Rocco James, their son (their very blond son, much like mine, whom I have no doubt would have been the source of a lot of ribbing between us, back and forth).

I imagine he would have been very successful. And by that I don't mean a best-seller. I mean a man who'd found satisfaction.

This project, this version of *The Garcia Boy*, would have thrilled him.

I can see that slow smile of his as he flips through the pages.

This is for you, *mi pana*, *mi hermano*.

And we can talk about what that means later.

Oh, what joy! Oh, what joy you've brought me, Emily.
What wonderful joy. With all my heart.

Here. This is for you.

PROLOGUE

My father likes to tell stories, and they may not always be true. While he riffs around one central idea, the characters and their motives always change, as do the scenes. He says things pell-mell, with no clear beginning, middle or end. He deals in the big themes, no matter how reckless his narrative may appear. He connects certain stories of our past with ideas from other times. There are no years associated with any of his stories. They happen in a time that can simply be known as "Yesterday." He talks about being a "Young Man," about a particular era he calls "Before America." These are some of the units by which he measures time in his stories. The other particular eras that stick out in my mind are: "Before My Father Was Murdered" and "Before Your Mother."

Like this: My father, Rafael Garcia, said to me one night a long time ago at his house in Romeoville, Illinois, far away from the hard, gritty streets of 19th and Damen in Chicago where he started his new American life more than 30 years ago, when I was still a drinker and we were on speaking terms, he said,

"Back in Mexico on the day my father was murdered, he was drinking. He must have been about 47. My mother didn't like him to drink too much because he was so crazy when drunk, but he did it anyway because he thought it was his right to do with his time whatever it was that he wanted to do. He gave her church on Sunday and she liked that and it seemed to lessen her wrath. It seemed to keep her less mad and crazy about things, about the drinking."

When my father tells these stories, he looks old. In the telling of these narratives it's clear he begins to wear the years he's consumed. Usually he's a man who laughs easily, cracks jokes and isn't afraid to use himself as the butt of gags or tricks if it elicits laughter from family and friends. He's a big man, a little over 6 feet with a stomach that has developed under the tutelage of savage alcohol abuse and reckless consumption of carne asada and rice and beans; needless to say, he's conscious of his ability to inspire fear. It's like a John Wayne Western; there's always a strict adherence to big ideas like honor, tradition and integrity, but there is always the possibility of unrest and pure violence. With every action taken and sentiment expressed, my father could save or he could terrorize.

The night he told me about the murder of his father, Ramiro, he wore sadness. While he told a story, it consumed him, and by the end of the night he became violent. Some event, some detail of memory, some random inner truth would strike him, and he would lash out.

My dad told me, "I thought he was so awful then, but I was such a young boy, being only 7 or 8 when he was murdered. I remember I never wanted to be hit by my father. *Mijo*, sometimes my memory is as bad as he was because I don't know sometimes if the man I am describing is really the man I knew."

Back in those days, on nights like that, my father told me that it didn't matter if the events or times lined up correctly in the story because it was the story itself that mattered, the center and the tragedy of it. Tragedy was and is the only thing that mattered.

He said to me, "Story is always the same, yes? It is always the same. It doesn't matter when or where. My father, your grandfather, was killed. Your Uncle Aurelio, your godfather, he killed the man who killed our father. That is the essential part of the story. I wish I knew more about my father. If I think hard about it now I cannot clearly see his face; more than that, I cannot see his sadness, but it must have been there, no? He's nothing but a cutout figure in my mind, my father. I love my father, but Rafa, he deserved every last nightmare and solitary moment. My saying this doesn't mean that I do not love him. It means that there are some things men deserve. Maybe his punishment is not being able to be seen clearly in my mind." My father tapped at his temples and looked at me, gauging if I understood exactly what he had said.

As my father talked, I thought about how he had consumed so much of my history even though I barely knew him, having been separated for many years by divorce and, ultimately, my own purposeful estrangement. I knew this for sure: My father and I liked to drink together. We shared the same sense of appreciation and recklessness that came with it. We shared the fight for it. The story (along with its implicit alcohol abuse) of my grandfather's death on February 9, 1964, never relieves me of my fascination with it. My father knows this. While he told me many stories, this one is the best. Before I got clean and sober, I loved him the most for this. I was once very far away from him, and then, through drinking and this idea of storytelling, I was very close to him and our kind. It was as if I had inherited a great artifact to employ in any way I saw fit. I learned about Mexico from my father and his stories. A place on the map before was then a place my father filled in with his words and these murders, my grandfather and his killer. This is how I learned about the place my father came from. This is how I learned about Mexico.

My dad continued: "You, too, will have one story that all the others will come from. You, too, will experience a tragedy that will give sense to that which was previously irrational. In this moment your stories will gain weight and sense. I had no stories before my father left. Now, I have many. I have a lifetime."

My Italian-American mother also tells me a lot about family origins, which are fueled by her memory, her idea of the past. She is very good with the truth. Rarely will I catch her telling me the same story in a different way. My mother remembers things according to the national events that surround them. While my father finds himself in personal tragedy, my mother loses herself in the telling of a story, as if her narrative voice becomes the narrative voice of America. She could be anyone, anywhere. She seems to be a passive observer in her own history, a kind of photographer. She is defined less by any tangible emotional force and more by a relentless subtext, the American collective subconscious.

Like this: On February 9, 1964, the same day my grandfather is shot dead in Mexico, 73 million Americans tune in to *The Ed Sullivan Show* at 8 p.m. Eastern Standard Time. My mother, Tari Torch, 16, a sophomore at Eastlake North High School in Ohio, is patiently waiting for what she and her friends have been talking about for a week now. They've discussed who their favorite is, John or Paul, George or Ringo. Some argue that John is the cutest, while others fight hard and tough for George or Paul, but Tari holds fast to Ringo because she thinks he's a sensitive boy with a nice smile, and being a little strange didn't hinder his cause. The others think she's crazy. John's a dream, they tell her. To be honest, Tari doesn't really care because she's a Rolling Stones fan at heart. She's wild about Mick Jagger.

Tari lives with her parents and two younger brothers in a ranch-style house out in Willowick, an eastern suburb of Cleveland. She has a boyfriend named Mike, the halfback for the football team whom everyone calls "Fireplug." Soon he'll go off to war in a place no one can find on a map, a communist country somewhere in Asia, from which he'll come back a messed-up alcoholic. One of Tari's brothers will go to Amherst College and protest the war. The other one, who is now only 6, will bear the brunt of their parents' eventual divorce and their mother's own horrific descent into alcoholism.

But for now, all that is far from my mother's mind. The Beatles are going to be on *Ed Sullivan* for their first American performance. Forty percent of the population will watch the man known as Mr. Television. He will corral a 60 share of the ratings.

Alone in her room, awaiting the broadcast and thinking of her future with Mike, my mother sings, "And when I touch you, I feel happy..."

My goal in writing about all this, my twofold inheritance, is to contemplate the ways in which we, as Americans, tell stories and the ways we begin to learn about our identities through the act of storytelling.

You see, more than skin color and cultural traditions, more than being "brown" in a white family and "white" in a brown family, I have inherited stories. Of course, it wasn't a thing I learned to wield overnight. I have had to reconcile the stories I've inherited. One could say that I am the heir to stories, but more than that, I have been given a way to read the world. In many respects, I have been made to not only explore the texts of my parents, but also become a kind of mapmaker in the process.

Living and teaching in the largest Mexican-American barrio in the Midwest, I've learned that the American narrative is never composed of just one story, memory or history. So along with examining the American experience through the lens of two families, one Mexican and one Italian, I want to explore it through the stories of other people—especially a kid who was killed, a kid who had the surname I did when I was born.

"The Garcia boy." That's what they still call him at the place where I teach, a Jesuit high school on the Southwest Side of Chicago with a variety of students, from gangbangers to kids who are the first in their families to go off to college. At the intersection of Mexican and American life, Cristo Rey High School, and the stories my students tell me there, has helped me to confront the very idea of America and the struggle of being "American."

I've discovered that what constitutes "American identity" is forever elusive and transforming. Back in Ohio in 1964, for instance, being American meant getting in the Chevrolet Impala and driving to your grandparents' house for Sunday dinner and *The Ed Sullivan Show*. See them now, my mother's family dressed up in their church best: a dress on Tari—although she hates it, she prefers jeans and a T-shirt—and nice shirts and slacks for her brothers, her dad in a tie. See them riding out along the manicured back roads of suburban Cleveland, the whole Torch family, with Tari looking out the window in her peach-colored dress, staring off into the distance. See her mother sprucing up her hair with the back of her hand, the slight bob she wears, a little something new, something in style.

The car motor working like a dream. Benny Goodman on the radio. The sun, the blue sky, the green lawns.

My father tried to put it into words. He said things like, "The old man turned around and staggered forward because he never fell into anything, Rafa. He was always on the precipice, always about to fall, his whole life.

"Ramiro told the other man to stand up. 'Stand up. Be a man,' he said. The old man's got his fists up. He must have looked funny. *Papi* was always all spitfire and loss."

My father listened closely to something in his imagination, something out of the past, his head tilted like he could hear better from one side. He nodded "yes," like he heard something true come out of the past, heard something true come out from the lies he was spinning. He lifted his bottle to his lips, took a couple of swigs from his beer and set it down.

When I was a practicing alcoholic, I told lies all the time. I lied in the name of stories. Thinking back, what I miss the most about drinking is the way I could craft a story, hold people spellbound with lies, like I was spinning a web. I don't know if it was a fascination with lying or fiction or a fascination with the idea of story. Drinking allowed me to share parts of myself that were blatantly untrue, but seemed to be true somewhere in me, therefore true and real. Watching my father, I was struck not by how any of this might be untrue, but by how beautiful he was as a storyteller. His body language, his use of space, his intonation, his use of silence. What struck me was not the truth at the core, but how easily he made me believe or forget that he was nothing more than a drunk telling me a story. Yeah, his father was murdered, but my own father's meanderings were splendid.

He was quiet for some time and then he said, "They swapped fists and bloodied themselves, kicked dirt into one another's eyes. This seems to have changed our family's destiny, if there is such a thing. Do you understand? This seems to be like how all men are changed. All history moves into and then out of these moments, yes? It is the only kind of history I know. It's bare bones and brutal, but true. Men move into conflict. Men move out of it, dead or alive.

"Maybe that's what happened that day when the strange man pulled his gun and pointed it into the face of my father who was stupid with drink. He must have just pulled the trigger and then lowered it, shot him in the chest, and then, finally, in the shoulder. Man pulls out gun. Man pulls trigger.

"My brother Aurelio and me came across him lying in the street, this man, my father, our father, a man I was so afraid of. I never knew he could look so small. I built him up so much in my mind, but he was only blood and guts and muscle and bone."

My father looked tired, beaten and wrecked. He paused, looked around his house, to the family pictures on the wall above his television, to the mirror with the image of the Last Supper superimposed on it. Finally, he said, "Aurelio left us and went to find that man. He killed him. *This* is the simple part. He just killed him."

My father banged his fist on the table. The empty beer bottles scattered. One fell to the ground and shattered into bits on the floor. He was not fazed. He looked at me long and deep and, as I bent down to pick up the large bits I could handle without the risk of being cut, he grabbed my wrist, pulled me to him, and said, "*This* is the simple part…the here…the now…there are the moments that happened afterward. There is Aurelio and the fear and murder in his heart. There is his time in jail. There is his leaving Mexico, many years later. My own running the border— an action born of the revenge, the incarceration of my brother. His own fear led to my own fear, which led me to here and your mother. Then there is you. It is not so simple after all, *mijo*. You are part of it. History has made you this way."

He let go of my wrist by flinging it to the side. I straightened up and stared at him. He picked up his bottle of beer and finished it off.

Thinking back to that night with my father before I quit drinking, I try to understand exactly what was said. In many ways it was a kind of birthright. It was something he had coddled for many years and told and retold, perfected in his own private self in order to tell me something about who he was and is. Yet none of this was about him personally. It was all about his father and my father, about fathers in general, that large, looming figure who dwelled in our minds longer than he dwelled in the physical world, standing over us, almost always about to thrash us. A man so muddled up by memory that there's nothing distinct left in the mind.

He was sweating. His hands shook. The night grew cold, and we moved on into our terrible drunkenness, my father and I, in our mutual silence and fear of one another out here in a town near Chicago in a place called the United States of America.

"Ladies and gentlemen, the Beatles!"

Ed Sullivan, the stoic, stone-faced impresario, points over to the stage and four boys with long hair and suits smile. The screaming in the audience is insane and even Tari, a Rolling Stones fan at heart, starts to scream. On the day Rafael Garcia finds his father dead in the street in a faraway place called Mexico, Tari Torch, his future wife and the mother of his firstborn son, is screaming, maybe crying, in America, her hands at her face because the Beatles are breaking out into song. It's all happening so fast. Listen to the voices and music moving out in waves over the vast American landscape. If you divide a still image into a collection of small colored dots, your brain will reassemble the dots into a meaningful image. History is in the white space. History is in the microdots that make up the images.

The Beatles sing, "Close your eyes and I'll kiss you. Tomorrow I'll miss you. Remember I'll always be true…"

1

THE GARCIA BOY

2003

The Garcia boy is gunned down on a dark street, somewhere in the 2700 block of South Hamlin, off the beaten path, early morning, a Sunday. *La Villita.*

Blood gurgles from his mouth. His body jerks and hiccups. He's been shot in the head and begins to think in strange, sporadic moments; time starts to jumble itself like if you took a reel of film and spliced it and put the scenes back together haphazardly and then ran them together with the sound out of sync. In my imagination, he's thinking in another kind of history, the shot-up kid. This close to death, the stories his memory manufactures are without beginning, middle and end. They lose their coherence, but, strangely, they make sense; they're tense with the kind of order death brings to the chaos of our lives. There, in the mixed-up and uncanny, the boy is true and real. His stories are coldly coherent and spot-on. He has other kinds of memory and story, this muted son of immigrants. Everything is confused and lost and yet maybe everything is just perfectly in its right place.

Somehow I can relate to the way he might have been thinking there, on the verge.

The kid, the Garcia boy, the wounded. The shot in the head and chest. He is me and I am him.

The Garcia boy looks as if he's sleeping with his eyes open. They glimmer for an instant, and then there's nothing and that spark he had in his eyes goes out, that spark I once knew when I was his American literature teacher and taught him about Jay Gatsby and J. Alfred Prufrock. His body goes limp like someone deflated him, took the air out of him. His pants go wet in the crotch.

Somewhere in the dark, the gunman runs out into the streets just beyond the shadows that are laid down by the neighboring playground, lightless homes and still-barren trees of early spring.

His two friends (one, the driver; the other, a passenger) are surrounded by the police in minutes. The blues and reds swirl over the houses, an ominous but usual sign. All's the same. Nothing's the same. A dead Mexican in the beaten-up back seat of a cheap car bought with someone else's savings.

The police radio it in. This is procedure. Standard operating procedure. Canvass the area. Talk to anyone. Knock on doors.

The people open and close their doors. Look out the shades, past their dirty curtains holding in the secrets of the hooligans in colors. They are a chorus from a Greek tragedy with their wordless mouths and veiled faces. They know everything. No one knows anything. *La Villita*.

I knew the Garcia boy for a few months, but it felt like years. Thinking back, I thought I had known him forever. There is much about him that I see in myself even now. The Garcia boy was a tall, lanky kid who was as awkward and clumsy as any 16-year-old boy.

Adolescence had the best of him. He was always leaning back in his chair, bored, biting his nails, nervous, almost falling out but not quite, a long foot wrapped around the desk leg. His bony, sick knees would scrape the edges of the desk and from there he would toss out an answer about Emerson. From there, near oblivion, he waxed poetic about Emily Dickinson or transcendentalism.

I force myself to remember that silly little face, all childhood and naiveté: a dab of grown-up somewhere around those high cheekbones and heavy, sleepy eyes, bored and musical.

I knew him both outside and inside the classroom, for he sat in my American literature class every day until he was shot dead, and then he was not in my class anymore. I knew him because I am the dean of students at his high school and he sat in my office or in the chair outside my door many days. When he died we left a seat open for him, but he never came back. He never came strolling in all cool and eager and complicated. He never came in chewing his pencil to the nub or joking with me. The Garcia boy just stopped coming to class.

Although I was never in a gang, I have had my fair share of troubles. I am a Mexican-American, originally from the neighborhood. I am 28 years old. I moved out of that neighborhood because of divorce. My parents just couldn't live together anymore. It never worked. While they moved on with their lives, I moved on with the memory of their marriage stuck down in the depths of me and all the little generational neuroses that plague future generations.

Gangs are the biggest problem I face as a teacher and dean. They are like the plague. No one can cure it and they are everywhere. These gangbangers stand at the corner, with their shaved heads and mean looks, cryptic stances and poses. They have gold chains, baggy pants and aggressive gestures. They hijack my neighborhood at night. They upend right and wrong. I am back after all these years to this neighborhood that was once my birthplace but today is sometimes little more than a war zone; a war between teenagers who carry semiautomatic weapons and kill each other because of an economic and psychological malaise they could not articulate if you asked them. It's all about honor, respect and loyalty to them. Here they are, look. I have tried to tell this story over and over again. In his death I may find a way.

He doesn't come into my classroom anymore, and I don't know if I am sad or happy about it. No more questions. No more answers. There are lots of little blank squares where check marks and grades should be. Everyone else has them except him. Oh yeah, he's dead, I think when I notice the absence of the symbols I've created to denote presence and completed assignments. I consider slashing his name with a pencil, driving a line right through him, but I think it might be a little sacrilegious. There are the days where I am lost to a kind of forgetfulness that I did not used to have. My memory used to be better, and I don't know if it is an effect of his death, the startling way in which it hit me, or whether I have ever been good at remembering the past and all the people that outline it and give it shape. So I leave his name alone. Today it is still there. His name and a history of missing assignments, tardies and absences. Then there is nothing.

The gangbangers are flashing signs at me more often now than ever before as if I were part of his life in some base way and they have smelled it out in me like dogs do the scent of another. Maybe it's something more complex they read in me, something in the eyes. I don't know.

Maybe they distrust my anger at them, the fury I have in my heart. Maybe it's the way I stand or manipulate physical space. I'm baldheaded and Fit-the-Description. I could stand with them. I could have been resting in the back seat, on the verge, if things had been made to be different, if my parents had reconciled.

I could sink in. Yet, I am a professional. I wear a shirt, tie, khaki pants and a sport jacket. I teach teenagers about literature and carry around lesson plans and grade books and syllabi. I have lectures that outline Marx's theory of alienation and illustrate Jesus' last temptation as an example of real anguish and platonic angst. I have subscribed to the American Dream, and the residuals have been fairly good. I live in a nice apartment with hardwood floors that are so highly polished that I could almost see myself in them if I got up close and tried to look.

Maybe it's always been this way in this tiny immigrant community on the Lower West Side of Chicago. Pilsen was once a gateway for people of Eastern European descent, the name itself a nod to all things Bohemian. It became a stronghold in the '60s as a strictly Mexican neighborhood, but for the better part of a century there have been Mexicans in this neighborhood, working and living, subscribing, either through virtue or vice, to the American Dream. Thousands of immigrants came here before settling into the Dream and all its dizzying complications and rewards. This neighborhood has changed the Mexicans—who believe so much in the Past—into people of the Future. It's a densely populated area, awash with newcomers and old-timers, well-oiled Americans still clinging, like it or not, to their Mexican identity.

It's the place where my father came after he finally made it to the United States many years ago, in 1972. After crossing the border, he traveled to Chicago where there were people he knew, friends of the family. There were hellish jobs, but jobs that paid better than the jobs in Mexico. Even today my father only knows how to work. It is the essential part of him. America afforded him the opportunity to devote all his time to the effort of filling out his essentiality. The man personifies work—even at the expense of the self. It is here that he spent the first five years of his American life (with us: my mother and me, an infant) before trying to make it in Cleveland with my mother and her family. My mother found it hard and constrictive to play the role some women play in Mexican culture—cooking, cleaning and moving in a bleak social scene. This was a culture totally alien to the one in which she was raised, the suburbs outside of Cleveland. She told him he needed to try living outside of the neighborhood. I think she hoped he would slow his drinking and drug use. She wanted so much more with this man who was only 21 and unable to give up all that he knew and be away from his people.

Pent-up and frustrated doing landscaping work for my grandfather (ironically, the son of an immigrant), who didn't particularly like Mexicans, especially those who married his daughter, my father left. He went back to Chicago on a Greyhound bus on Christmas Eve 1977. He called my mother at a pay phone and told her, "I can't do it anymore."

She said, "Okay." And that was it.

In a conversation filled with silence, they assented to the possibility that their marriage was a mistake, a great failure. They didn't say as much, but they knew. Each realized in that moment that while their love for one another was real and true, they married because each was rebelling from the very thing that had gotten them to that point: their upbringing; for my father, being the son of a poor rancher's son and for my mother, being the daughter of a football coach and schoolteacher in white, middle-class America. They were actively rebelling against the passion of time and history and the inability for any of us to totally shear ourselves away from it. I was born of a passion, the offspring of rebellion. I was the active creation of a resistance so human and so foolish that it would make one cry and wail if it weren't so natural to what it is that makes us human.

My father told my mother, "I can't do this anymore, Tari."

She said to him, "I will raise Rafa. Please. You will have to stay away."

It was snowing in Chicago where my dad called from. When it was all said and done, my father hung up the pay phone, paused with his hand on the receiver and then let go. He stepped out of the phone booth, flipped his collar up and walked out of our lives, into the deep, dirty snow, leaning into and against an angry and piercing Chicago wind.

Days after the Garcia boy was gunned down in Little Village, I was driving down 18th Street to drop off rental videos. The weather had broken and the sun was hot. For the first time in many months the streets were alive. A distinct fiesta feeling had come back to the neighborhood after a long, hard Chicago winter. Windows were rolled down and people hung from their second- and third-floor flats, out over the fire escapes; laundry swung in the alleys and gangways. Old people had brought out the lawn chairs. Children ran in and out of the street between cars, riding scooters, chasing friends, their chants and cries reverberating around the neighborhood and the alleys. Their sentences are compact and full of life, powerful in the dual nature of the words, weighed down by two languages: that of their parents and the one they found in their schools and on television, the one they began to mine behind their parents' backs.

Young men drank in the shadows out on the streets and on their stoops. It was these warm weather days of early spring that were the most dangerous. An uncertainty hung in Pilsen, the possibility of explosion that had brought people into the street. It bordered on violence and pure joy.

I was at a stoplight. My window was rolled down; something in me wanted to feel a part of it. Somewhere down this street, I began to feel at home, here, with these people. My radio was turned up and the rock and roll came coursing out of the speakers and into the street.

"Hey, *vato. Qué pasa?*" I heard from my left.

I stared straight ahead and the familiar pain came to me. Deep in the stomach it started. Somehow I felt guilty. It was as if I were a member of the rival gang. Deep inside, I was a Latin King, a Satan Disciple, a Vice Lord, a Two Six boy, an Ambrose. In my mind, I wore the Pitchfork. I painted inverted pitchforks over upright pitchforks. I wrote on the walls of the stalls in public restrooms and the garages of the neighborhood in the black of night—KING LOVE. The same act I expelled students for, I produced and envisioned for myself. I was a five-pointed crown. It all came back to me. I was guilty.

"Hey, *vato.*"

I looked over and two guys stared at me from the shadows of the steps leading into the apartments above. One had a beer in his hand and his head was shaved. The other was tall, his face a mix of sharp, almost geometric features. He looked ancient and primal, standing there in the shadows, half in and half out. Their clothes were clean and pressed. Perfect gold crucifixes hung from their necks. The drinker was short and squat. They were like middleweights, wound-up bundles of energy waiting to be propelled forward. Together they were a battalion of hate and pent-up frustration.

"*Qué necesitas*, homes?" the short, ferocious one asked before he sipped his beer, cool and calm. The other reached underneath his shirt, into the waistband of his pants, for something violent. The short one threw a cold, incoherent hand symbol into the air.

People near them slowly scattered like children who had spilled or broken something. They moved away, almost nonchalantly, because anything else the *gangueros* would smell and pounce on. They neither wanted to be feared or not feared. These gangsters wanted something impossible, and the people obeyed. The whole neighborhood dwelled in the impossible. The speakers at a secondhand store blared Mexican music. Everyone around me knew this sign, the hand signal he'd thrown in the air. I looked in the rearview mirror and the woman in the car behind me rolled up her window. People looked for exits.

I said, out my window into 18th Street, to everyone almost, announcing, proclaiming, conceding, "I'm just passing through." It amounted to retreat. More to myself than anybody else, I said, "I'm just passing through."

Ironically, I could get by because I didn't speak any Spanish. There was no accent riding my words, pulling them down. I was more white boy than *vato*. I hated myself. I wanted to rub the white boy from me with a scouring pad.

My adversary said, backing up with his hands in the air, "Cool, *ése*, cool."

There was a certain amount of wisdom in his words. He had no idea who I was. Did he take a shot? Did he risk it or go back into the shadows of the sunny day, take a sip of Tecate and roll on with his homies? In his world, I was another *ganguero*, what with my shaved head and a something-else he recognizes, or I was an undercover in an unmarked car. Either way I was a deception he was not ready to face down or try to understand. Everyone in the guy's life was an either/or. He was caught up in a series of deceptions. Either one was in the rival gang or one was a cop. His whole life was a series of these kinds of risks. This brown kid living in a black-and-white world he'd created for himself—born of paranoia and fear.

The tall, sharp one moved backward onto the sidewalk, him and his mean, cloudy eyes and tough cowboy posture, some ancient pose made for all the right and wrong reasons.

I couldn't speak Spanish, but I was drawn in by skin color, dark eyes, a shaved head and an ancient braggadocio, something brought over the border by my father and his; something brought over that has everything to do with suspicion and scorn for self and others who may confuse my own vision of what the self could be.

I often dream about the gurney being rolled out of a misshapen ambulance, an inferno of sorts with all the red lights and wires, medical boxes of noise. In the dream, the paramedics roll the gurney toward the car where the Garcia boy sits slumped in the back seat of the Chevy. I see taut yellow police tape wound around the trees that border the street, forming a wide perimeter. The dull light of the sky comes down around the place, setting everything ablaze in a white glow.

Delicately, they heave him up onto the stretcher. There are howls and jeers from the people who are half asleep in their robes and undershirts. Men smoke cigarettes. Women pray or stare.

Someone says, "Make way. Make way."

They take him to the ambulance. The stretcher hits the end of the car and the wheels give out and they wheel him up into it. They work under a bright white light, looking down on the kid. Medical workers attempt to revive the juvenile. It's a done deal though. They go through the motions. They do CPR. One guy has blood on his hands. Another guy makes a joke. Someone laughs. A medic writes on a clipboard, checks his watch and writes something down. They hook the Garcia boy up to things and speak sentences full of clean, glossy English, and there's a crowd around the back of the vehicle and sometimes I cannot see into the ambulance and this worries me. I cannot see the Garcia boy, all the dead weight and bloody clothes, soiled shoes and those crisscrossed eyes. I am not in the crowd but I am, and this worries me because I wonder how I am seeing things so sharply, so clearly.

I think I hear myself yell, "He's dead. Put a fork in him. He's done." No one hears me, of course. "He's dead," I tell no one at all.

I hear detectives talk to beat cops. One sips coffee. Steam rises. He's shot in the chest. Shot in the head. The boy's a plain message to someone in some other hood or gang. He's a billboard now. An advertisement.

Three or four detectives search the pavement for spent slugs. They wear powdered rubber gloves, and their silk ties are tucked into their shirts to avoid the puddles of blood that have pooled around where they are crouched looking for clues, signs and symbols. Innocent bystanders hover near the yellow tape, one with a blanket around her shoulders. They are shivering in the chill.

His eyes are closed. White sheets are draped over the boy, now a corpse. Blood moves like syrup into the rifts and ruts in the road. Even though I know it is him being gathered up and shuffled into the back of the vehicle, in the dream I can't help but see myself lying on the stretcher. I am telling them, "I am not dead. I am not dead." Yet no one hears my voice. I am dead and I am not. They pull a white sheet over him, and I struggle under the white sheet, flailing because it's hard to breathe under here, under all this death. And then I wake up and lie awake and motionless for hours, struck dumb. That's usually how it goes these nights that bleed into morning.

Though he sat in my class for only five months, he's as mysterious to me now as ever before. He's more real when imagined deep in my brain. Somewhere in the dark he must have resembled somebody important to the Latin Kings. He's an omniscient symbol hanging over everyone lost in the dark.

Then again, maybe it wasn't a terrible mishap. Maybe the Garcia boy was for real, a made man, a Two Sixer—the rival gang that is named for the street which they haunt, 26th Street. Maybe this was always going to happen to the Garcia boy. It wasn't about how it was going to happen, but just a matter of time before it did. And there I am under my covers, sweating and shaking, coming out of the dream I've been in for what seems like a million years, all naive and hopeful, the dreamer I am.

Maybe he wasn't a made man, I think, turning the shower on, letting the cold turn to hot. Maybe he wasn't a Two Six boy, I think, these days, sitting up alone in my bed strangely tense with doubt and fear. "Maybe it was a case of mistaken identity," I say when I am in the shower soaping up and rinsing off. I say it with a mouthful of toothpaste, putting shaving cream on and running the razor over my face and then, later, eating cereal, doing the dishes, feeding my cats. I tell my cats, mewing at my legs, hungry and indifferent to the politics of identity, I say, "Being from the neighborhood, I think it was a little of both." In these days in the wake of the murder, on the bus on the way to work down Cermak, I say out loud like some stunned derelict, "Yeah. It was a little of both."

By the time my dad was 21, he was married, had a kid, a steady job. His brother Aurelio had come, his sisters, too. There was a steady rise in the number of family members coming to the States, escaping a violent family past rich with lore. In Pilsen, my father found a common identity with others like him, heavy drinkers, drugs he began to use and sell, marijuana and cocaine, outlets to make a little money on the side. A package here, a package there. Don't ask. Don't tell. These were the first great mottos of my father's American life, an American life where money went fast but was easy to come by. An America where anything and everything you wanted was right here, all the truths in front of you, if you could make them out, decipher them.

In a steam room in an old Russian shvitz on the North Side of Chicago many years before I got sober, my father introduced me to a few of his friends whom he ran with back in the late '70s, before and after my mom left him. They were rough men with gold chains and deep tans. They all told me, like a mantra of working-class, ethnic solidarity, "If you need anything, anything, you call me. A son of Rafael's is a friend of mine." They smiled, shoved me around a little. I looked at my dad and he smiled, swelling with pride. "He's a smart, good-looking kid, your *hijo*," they told my dad after I told them about college, about my desire to be a teacher one day.

Myself, I was awed by the attention and praise showered on a man I really only knew through his drunk phone calls when I was a boy and by the exaggerated half-truths my mother told me about him. I was stunned to think he had this other life. It was obvious who these men were, what they stood for. Them standing like kings in a men's club, doling out the 20s, buying beer for everyone. Their expensive Italian shoes, their cashmere sweaters and Rolex watches.

My father told me, pointing to one of the men, "He's a big dealer. He moves heavy amounts of cocaine." The man was throwing copious amounts of water on the stones to make the room even hotter than it already was.

"How do you know him?" I asked, the steam making our faces red and weary.

"I just do."

We drank so much that night, my father and I. We drank beer and then tequila and then more beer. After the steam rooms, we sank into ice-cold pools of water and then we drank more.

After we left my father asked, "Do you want to see where your mother and I lived when you were little?"

"Yeah, okay."

We drove to a beautiful house on a little street. We were drunk. We sat in the car looking up into the place like undercover agents, secretly taking back memories. Me making them up, my father remembering a simpler time, a time when he was younger and in love with a woman who infuriated him and was so madly different than he was. But that was the point, I guess, for him.

Love, for my father, was never an easy thing. It was something that tore people down, ate them up and spit them out. He said, looking up into the windows of the house, the whole neighborhood a gentrified version of the past, great big loft spaces now, white people in them, "I loved your mother." He said it twice more, each one a rehabbed version of the last. He tried out a different voice each time. He laid it out there. It was almost a question. Something about it made me think he needed me to confirm him, it, the thing said. It was strange and weird and cold, and I looked at him.

"Yes. I know," I told him, looking from him to the street before us. I don't know this for sure, but I felt like I couldn't let him down.

The neighborhood had changed from when we lived there. Geraniums now hung from windowsills. There were community watch signs. It was silent, this place, the house in front of us that meant something different for each of us, for him, my mother, me, something unknown, but possible.

"Yes," he said, uncomfortable with the confession, pushed on by drink. He said, "I loved her more than anything. I think I might still love her, *mijo*." He stared straight ahead and grabbed my head and tousled my hair like I was 10 years old. His hands were large and swollen with work. He didn't wear his wedding ring anymore, the ring that symbolized his marriage with the woman he had met after my mom, a Mexican woman from his village; he didn't wear the ring anymore because his fingers were so big and work-worn. Looking at his hands, I was terrified. His work had squandered him, and sitting with him that night, I watched him peruse the past. Whether or not it was true what he was thinking, I noticed the years that had passed him by and all the drunkenness that had followed him to all the places he had gone.

Finally, breaking the silence, my father told me, "I need a beer. You?"

We drove to a place around the corner, a small hole in the wall, a little bar with a small window, bars up around it and a neon sign that said "Cold Beer." We opened the door and walked in and there were five or six people there, all regulars.

We were drunk and took two stools near the end of the bar, which was dark and smelled of pickles, stale beer and cigars. The jukebox was loud and the television louder. My father and I ordered beers, and we stared at the tube hanging from a corner at the far end of the place. We sank into our own little stories we had for one another. We realized there was nothing else to say, or worse, that neither of us was really working hard at trying to know the other. Finally, he said, "Here. He gave this to me to give to you."

I looked down into his hand, which was under the bar. In his palm was a little baggie filled with white powder. I looked at my dad and he looked at me, dead drunk, his eyes like a rat's, black and watery, his face bloated. I took the baggie, looking around. I mumbled, "Thanks," and put it into my jacket.

He nodded and looked into the mirror running along the length of the bar where the bottles of liquor were. We drank.

After a long, rough silence, I said, "Got to go to the bathroom."

With a touch of sarcasm, he slurred, "Okay. Bathroom. Yeah, go to the bathroom, *mijo*." He smiled strangely, still staring at himself in the mirror.

In the bathroom, I sank into the stall. I opened the baggie and dabbed my finger into the powder and then licked it. It was coke, all right. I sat back and wondered if this was a dream, my father giving me cocaine in a bar he used to drink in when he was married to my mother who hated his alcoholism and who hated mine. I doled a little out onto the meat of my left hand between thumb and forefinger and bent my head down to take it all in. I did that a couple of times and sat there and waited to get high. There in that place, that shitty bar where my father was out there drinking it all away, this American life. And me, his oldest son, sniffing it all up his nose, his gift, this American life.

I thought I heard Bill Withers' "Ain't No Sunshine" from the jukebox. The jukebox said, "I know I know I know I know I know I know..."

It had only been a week. The Garcia boy's seat. Empty.

Some other teacher, a priest who shared the room with me, had written "Know Thyself" on the board, and I refused to erase it so I wrote things around it. I wrote, "For Gatsby it was borrowed time anyway." They wrote it down and then I wrote, "Valley of Ashes." And they wrote it down. I wrote, "Imagery of Nature. What is Nature?"

I looked at Maria Guerrero[1], the Garcia boy's best friend, his desk mate, and I said, "This is the how the world ends. Not with a bang but with a whimper." She looked down, back at her notebook, back at her text. I hadn't asked her a question, but she looked for answers. Maybe she was looking down to avoid the logic of the sentences.

I wondered what he would have thought of that. He was quite a student, average on paper, but he had a terrific mind. His test scores—1300 SAT—indicated a mind we would defend as educators. The kid didn't study, but he was one of those kids I would have been jealous of when I was in high school. He was the kid who screwed off in class, but when a teacher came down on him or asked the real important questions like, "What's the nature of Twain's humor?" or, "Why is Moby Dick white?" he

1. With the exception of Sergio Garcia, all names of Cristo Rey students in this book are pseudonyms.

would pipe up with some passionate answer to move the class toward the light.

The bell was going to ring. They would pick up their books and some would look at me and say goodbye, and I would say goodbye back to them and then they would leave the classroom. The bell rang. I told them, "We are not done."

They looked at me. I wrote on the board, around the "Know Thyself" bullshit, nonsensical things. I wrote, "Mr. Nobody From Nowhere. An Isolated Figure. A mysterious and ambivalent figure." I wrote, "Gatsby's past and his destruction." In my messy scrawl, I wrote, "Dead. In death he found himself again."

The Garcia boy wrote, in a Write-a-Poem-Using-Emily-Dickinson-Themes assignment days before his death:

> As if it were measured out
> perfect, step by step, piece by piece like blueprint,
> all planned out Death unfolds.

With the wake and the funeral, I hadn't had a chance to grade these poems for many weeks. When I read these first few lines, they left me vacant. I wanted to go and find his grave, dig him up, and pull his dead body up by the shirt collar and yell, "What did you know, kid?" He had seen so much death in his neighborhood. He knew it was only a matter of time. Maybe he saw it in the neighborhood noises that filled his days: yelling children, the secret clichéd mutterings of old, Catholic women and the handful of pious men, the chorus of guns, automatic and semi. Maybe he sensed it in the mindless way he and his homies cruised up and down 26th Street, looking for that one guy who looks at him the wrong way. His poem is not Dickinson, but it's complete and truthful. I gave him an A even though he was dead.

The kid wrote:

> *Sudden, yet without a sound*
> *To so many beautiful things, the end*
> *Slowly coming*
> *Death unfolds.*

When I was 6 or 7, there were scary phone calls in the middle of the night. There were drunken phone calls in the early morning, sometimes in the late afternoon. My father would call to speak with me, or, if my mother wouldn't let him, he would tell her he was coming to get me. He would tell me that my mother was keeping me from him. He would ask me, if I was able to come to the phone, "Don't you want to come and live with me?" He would say, "You could do anything you wanted here."

This was attractive. My father had begun to seem like Mr. Nice Guy. I got good at using this against my mother when she was angry with me. If she sent me to my room, I would say from the threshold, half in my room and half out, knowing full well that if I stepped fully out my mom would come at me like a woman possessed, "I'll go live with my dad." I said it like an expletive. I stabbed her with it, tried to pierce her heart. It was thrown like a homemade bomb, recklessly, pitched out, hoping not for a direct hit but as much damage as possible.

She would reply coolly, tongue-in-cheek, "Go ahead. Good luck, Rafa." She would go about her business, studying for tests she had when she was still in school, before it got to be too hard as a single mother to juggle me, her work, school and a social life that might allow her the company of another. My mom knew better, having lived with my father long enough to know about broken promises. She would tell me, "Go ahead, Rafa. Go live with your father. You'll see. One of these days you will see. You will know."

She would shoot me a look and then turn her attention back to her books. Her stare was enough for me to believe her. My mother never said anything terrible about my father. Coming to know him on my own terms was very important to her. But she knew I would find out not just the bad but also the good. I watched her all those nights, slaving away at her books, cooking me dinner, falling asleep on the couch before me because she was so tired. She was a beautiful woman, what with her brown hair, slender body, small frame and a biting, almost brooding, sense of humor born of the pain of the previous decade. She should have been being loved and loving beyond the intensity with which she loved me. Thinking back now, I realize how hard it must have been to be in her early 30s and single, raising a boy who was so much like the man she left, a young boy with the same deep, brown eyes and black hair and walk and hands as his father. "Go ahead, Rafa. Go live with him," she would say to me, a slight chuckle at the end of her words.

It seemed so impossible, him and her as a couple. He was an impossible idea. My father was either something to hide from or hide behind. For much of my childhood, rather than a human being, he was a concept to consider. He was an explanation for all the things that could go wrong in my life, but there was also something about his presence and all the absence of it that allowed him to become the promise of something I could not yet figure out. What was it? Why hide from him or behind him?

Sometimes, in a loud voice, my mother would say, "Never call here again," or in a soothing voice, quiet and unashamed, "Please, Rafael. Don't make this hard." She would say, sometimes, "You're drunk. I won't talk to you when you're drunk."

I remember the phone calls as prologues to a wider dialogue with my father, the phone calls where he would call and threaten or try to make good again, show us he had become (or would become) a better man. They introduced me to a man who was capable of forgetting earlier stories in order to make up new ones, a man who was capable of reinventing a future (however impossible) he dreamed up for us.

My mother would later say to my grandmother, weary and morose, "He's trying to get sober. He says he's getting better. He's sick." Did she believe him when she said things like that behind closed doors? Did she picture herself in the new story?

There was the time he told us he was dying. He told her, "I have kidney problems." He was looking for sympathy from a woman he loved, maybe still loved. "I'm dying. I need you here for when I die. I need my son here. He needs to know his father before I die." (Father comes home. Father spends sunset of life with wife and child. Holding hands. Picnics. Bucolic sunsets and kisses, tousling the boy's hair. "Hey there, Sport." Dies early, but dies having erased the worst part of history.)

My mother said smartly and plainly, "Quit drinking, Rafa. You aren't dying. You know the cure. You always have." This phrase, Quit Drinking, the familiar fix my mother always had, the advice she always gave to him and, later in life, to me. It was always about the drinking, always about inebriation. It was always, for my mother, about getting sober. Sober: habitually abstemious in the use of alcoholic liquors or drugs. Sober: devoid of exaggeration or speculative imagination.

There was an essentialness to the Garcia boy, some kind of deeper understanding of the world around him that drew me to him. He had a confidence at his center that most of the other kids did not. There were other gangbangers in the school for sure. There were other kids knee-deep in the muck, but the boy had something: a vision of himself in the world. He understood tragedy at its core, whether or not he could articulate it purposefully in any way. The propensity for crime was always present, but there was an ironic playfulness with it that one could detect in his body movements, his thrust of self in the world. One can only guess at the things he did out on the street; yet the loping, almost drunk appeal of the world for him suggested a dirty, mysterious affair with irony. How could the kid understand his role and the system he adhered to without finding an ironic pleasure in the seeking out of crime? What was it, this mystery, this fabulousness of crime and the glitter and hopped-up glamour of it, his self-guided tour of the streets and violent memories of past war and attack, past celebration and tribal joy? What was it about the fiction he had created about himself, being in a gang, wielding "power," that he found so enjoyable?

Only months before the Garcia boy's death, I called him into my office to talk with him about his grades. I also began to talk, informally, about his plans for the future. It was tough talk for an urban teenager. I asked him, "What are you going to do with your summer?" It was no idle question, as it's common knowledge that these boys need something to do in the summer to keep them away from the voluptuous appeal of the street. The streets were sexy and solicitous. For the Garcia boy, it was no different.

I had recommended a summer program at the College of William & Mary. It was a three-week, intensive study program focused on the earliest social communities of American history, places where tough immigrants weathered the worst of their new American lives and the sudden loneliness of their new land, a newfound solitude. I showed him the information, and although he was a bit turned off by all those happy white faces and drummers and fife players of Colonial Williamsburg, he seemed into it.

He looked at the pictures, looked at me, and pointed out, "They're all white." Being amid all those white people may have been odd and possibly unnerving. He looked up for a moment and then, looking back to the text, smiled.

"Yes. They are. They're white," I said. "They don't bite, though."

He laughed. I laughed. He continued to stare at the pictures. His eyes moved slowly across the glossy surfaces. He turned the pages delicately. He touched the very edges of the top corners like it was poison, slowly turning page after page.

White kids holding pre-Betsy Ross flags, dressed in the rigid black-and-white of the ferocious Salem he read about in *The Crucible* only months earlier. For him, the book was the only representation of white folks in early America.

"They look like the characters in that Miller book," he said. "Weird. Is everyone like that?"

"What do you mean?"

"Are all white people like that?" He pointed to a young man dressing and acting like a woodworker, making special purpose squares and bevels to work in awkward locations, building wood houses. "Would I have to do this? I mean, there weren't even Mexicans then, right?"

"No, you won't have to dress up like colonial people. You study. You study them. You study *it*."

Still, I knew that somewhere inside him he thought that if he went there, this might mean he would abruptly become white like all the teenagers lighting gas lanterns along the dirt roads of Williamsburg, Virginia. In many ways, I think this is why he didn't study, why others like him don't either; he felt that it might sell him out. Somewhere learning became a beeline for the white man's world, a way to move from the ethnic enclave into the wider world where they have learned from revisionist textbooks. The white man oppresses, dominates and squanders. Leaving home intellectually means selling his people out. Looking at the book, the smile on his face told me he didn't believe that he could ever go there and belong. It was a fiction. The smile on his face showed me he'd never board that plane and take up residence in Williamsburg.

He told me over and over again he wanted to go, but he was fooling me. He was great at giving party lines. He grew up having to give them to parents, police and other gangbangers in the hood. He was a born liar, out of survival at first and habit second.

There were hints and rumors swirling about that he was involved in gangs, was a made man. Over the pictures and program descriptions set out in black and white, over the grand pullout picture of a white girl jubilantly holding onto the ropes of a colonial schooner in Chesapeake Bay, I looked for violent traces somewhere in his eyes. I wondered what this 110-pound little boy could do to anyone out on the street. He couldn't pull a gun, sell drugs or hold a neighborhood hostage. The kid could barely stand it if I told him to shut up in class when he talked too much with his friend Maria. I looked for any sort of tense muscle under all the sinew and bone of his forearms and the long, strange hands, innocent and vaguely feminine. I looked for bruises or any telltale mark on his neck that would divulge promiscuity or "walking the line," the initiation period where the novitiate takes a beating from his "brothers" for a short period of time.

He was always vague about his associations, vague about his whereabouts, vague about who he was. I should have asked him outright. But we didn't do those things then, pre-emptive strikes at a kid's character. Things were different before he died. But die he did.

I should have given him the hard evidence of my life, which was there in my eyes staring at him if he just looked at me seriously for one moment, deeply and without shame. He would have seen it: a ferocious alcoholism, the cocaine, the fistfights, broken noses, guns, my mother crying because she woke at the sounds of sirens in the middle of the night thinking, "He's dead," the ruined and forlorn jail cells in which I learned the hard way. Free. I would have given it for free. We could have moved past all the personal innuendos of history and the uncomfortable formalities of personal revelation. I suppose I could have and should have, but I just didn't do it because I didn't know how to say it then. And I didn't really know who he was yet. It was he who allowed me to see who I was. But he had to die for me to see, to witness and to perceive.

Careening out of control, my father took the highway's long curves at high speeds, moving in and out of lanes, bumping cars, smashing into guardrails, the lights of Chicago shimmering in the winter night, the city like glass, an object to be taken and broken. He propelled himself at 80 miles an hour, sometimes over 100 on the straightaways. Over dotted yellow lines, white lines, headed for exits and then back onto the highway in long, dangerous swerves, tires screaming, axles moaning. It was 2 a.m. and the cop cars followed at a safe distance, their sirens wailing like a requiem. In the night, their lights were like ghosts against the concrete at the side of the freeway. He was howling drunk. Handcuffed and haranguing in Spanish and English. My father bent his head as he was forced into the police cruiser. He yowled and cried out. He leaned back in the bucket seats of the Chicago police car and kicked at the windows, a man without a country, a man broken and beaten, a drunk in the back seat of a car, kicking at the windows, yelping for freedom with each new kick, "It's not me. *Yo no soy el que Ustedes están buscando.*" In a certain slant of light, he could see himself in the reflection, kicking and screaming. He stopped kicking, sat up and said, more to the reflection of himself than the cop looking at him through the window, he said, "It's not me. I am not the man you are looking for."

The kid who never did his homework, the Garcia boy, wrote:

> *Fearless evil in the night.*
> *Never still, always dancing rhythmically to a mysterious melody*
> *And never, single insight to what its plan could be*
> *Death unfolds.*

Driving home one night from an 18th Street Mexican restaurant, I talked to my mother on my cellphone. She told me I should move away from where I lived. I looked out the window, out into the streets. They were illuminated by a broad refulgence, like an urban aurora. The lights dazzled over the wet concrete. She said, as I looked at old brick three-story flats with fire escapes running along the fronts and sides of buildings, the dark alleys and deep gangways like open wounds, "I'm worried about you, Rafa. I don't like all that gang stuff. It's like the Wild West. It reminds me of your father and the recklessness of his brothers. Move away."

I told her, "It's okay. Nothing is going to happen to me."

"I just don't know what I would do if anything happened." Then she said something I couldn't make out as I looked back out into the Mexican-American night.

Because my parents divorced when I was an infant, I had no memory of my father until I was 12. My mother and I had been visiting her brother in Dayton, Ohio, and when we were leaving she asked me suddenly, "Do you want to go to Chicago to see your father and your family?"

In the fogginess of memory, I remember agreeing to it, unsure and vaguely scared, but charged by the possibility of a place called Chicago, by a father whose voice haunted me from phone calls and whose face was the microdots of color piled together in pictures, a heap of saturation, a stain on a piece of paper. He was, until that point, two-dimensional. He was merely the raw tension of a narrative my mom told. He was a literary device, either a mark of time or a vehicle for thematic exploration. He was the quesadillas and enchiladas my mom made, the guacamole she threw together when I was a child. He was the country I chose to write about in sixth grade for a project called "Mexico: My Father's Country." He was all the cultural traditions my mother trained me to know. He was the epic story of estrangement.

We drove all day and near dusk we passed Gary, Indiana, which was nothing but low brick buildings and ugly skies. We drove toward the first of Chicago certainties in the distance— Lake Michigan, a dark blue abyss, and the faint skyline, all shadow and conjecture. To the west, buildings and machinery, the hinterlands of progress, the secret world of American Might. We saw signs that said "Chicago Skyway." It was steel bridges and smoke. It was dirty, man-made clouds, rough homes and barren, gray places.

My mother said, "Here it is. Chicago." She was excited and singsongy about it.

Looking at my mother, I saw her see it all again for the first time. It had been a little over a decade since she left here, since the divorce. All the noise of the Dan Ryan, all the traffic, all the red lights and horns, heavy industrial parks out in the distance. Bombed-out tenement buildings. The Sears Tower out there, high up against the sullen, early night and pink and purple sky, stained and imaginary. Somehow, even at 12, I knew I was home. This place felt right.

My mother said, "What do you think?"

"I don't know yet." I shrugged. "It's a lot to take in."

She laughed. "Now we have to figure out how to reach him.

He has no phone, apparently. We'll have to call your Aunt Challo. She'll know how to get ahold of him. She'll freak out. They're going to be really excited." She patted me on the leg and charged ahead. "Don't worry," she told me, her eyes on the road ahead. "They love you."

At a gas station off the highway, my mother got out of the car and walked to a pay phone. I watched my mother smile and laugh and gesture madly. She was talking to someone she knew, someone happy to hear from her, happy to know she was here in Chicago. It had been a long time, but the way my mom moved, the gestures she produced, illustrated a long ache for another time and place, a whole decade worth of ache and wonder about a life she had left behind in history.

Darkness came over the sky. Soon we were driving off the highway onto little side streets, in what I would later learn was Pilsen. The streets seemed to hold their breath, crowded and urgent. My mother couldn't reach my father, of course, but my aunt had told us not to worry. She said she would see to it that he knew I was coming and that we should just come to her house as soon as we had gotten settled at our motel. Crawling along over the tiny streets, my mother asked, "Are you excited?"

"Yeah. I guess. Will he be there?" I was maybe secretly wishing he wouldn't be, afraid of him in my heart. Guilty because of it. Even in recent years, when I'd go over to see him, I have experienced the same feeling, half excited, half tearful. What would I have to say to him? How could we catch up after such an absence? What stories would we tell?

I looked out into the gangs of kids moving, rambling over the streets. Ahead, on 19th Street, the street my aunt lived on, there was a massive swelling of people, men with cowboy hats, woman laughing, kids everywhere, a whole blast of bodies and language, music from somewhere. My mother said, "Oh my God."

"What?" I asked, looking out into the street ahead. There were dozens of people, scores of bodies.

"That's them. That's your family." My mom pointed ahead to the people, to the mob. "This is crazy." She laughed and couldn't seem to believe her eyes. "It's not surprising though. Here they are, Rafa. Get ready."

Bodies overtook the car. There were hands and torsos, heads without frames behind other forms and shapes. Kinsmen, a tribe of citizens. My mother said, "Holy shit."

I looked out into the crowd, searching for the man I knew from pictures, this guy called "Dad." Smiling faces spoke Spanish. My mother parked the car. And standing near the gate leading to my aunt's flat was my father, a big, cagey man who was tall and everything expected, everything dreamed. He leaned so cool and my mother laughed and they hugged.

Someone yelled, "*Un beso. Un beso.*" My father blushed. People applauded when my mother kissed his cheek. Their intimacy, while uncomfortable, wasn't forced. It was natural and loving. My mother's hands on his shoulder were enough to show me a love that was very real and true. Then she said, pulling me to her, "This is Rafael."

He put out his hand. I put out mine.

People laughed and pointed at the father and son. The family converged, the whole thick melting pot of it. They overtook us and, all of a sudden, my mom was somewhere else, out of the picture. All these brown people and brown faces and foreign names. They were patting me on my back, introducing themselves, muttering things to me that I couldn't make out, moving back into the mass behind me.

My father said, "Hey." After 12 years, he said, "Hey." His hand moved over my face to my shoulders. He was making sure I was all there, the kid he once knew. He pounded my back. Big heavy hands, all raw knuckles and thick skin.

I said, "Hey." He led me upstairs to the party. All night people took pictures and told crowded, hurried histories, too much to tell, too much to say, not enough time. My father drank beer and stayed away and then came close, moved away again, shocked by my presence. My mother was with the women in the kitchen again, turning tortillas, drinking beer and gossiping.

A decade. What is a decade of loss and separation?

My father took me out onto the fire escape to leave the configuration of family and he said, "Tell me everything. Don't hold back. Tell me everything you know. What have you done?"

I began and then stopped. "School," I said. "Lots of school. I don't know." What was I supposed to say? I was 12 years old.

He laughed, said, "I miss you."

"Yeah. Me too," I said because I felt like I had to. I didn't know if I did and I felt uncomfortable saying it. I felt like I stabbed my mother in the back.

The fire escape looked out on 19th Street, below people and cars, neon lights, and out over the houses, there was Chicago. After some uncomfortable silence, he said, "Here. Take this." He took off a gold ring that was on his right-hand ring finger. It was a huge thing, shiny and heavy. In the center of the ring, there was a big R of diamonds. He said, "It's all yours now."

"Cool," I said. He smiled, chuckled, put it on my finger and drew me to his large frame.

We stood that way for a time before he let me go again.

2

NEW AMERICANS

2003

Lately, even before the shooting of the Garcia boy, but worse now, Maria Guerrero has taken to staring out over the rooftops during class. She sits with her legs crossed, her soft green eyes searching the tops of houses and businesses along Cermak. Maria was a friend and desk partner of the Garcia boy, and Maria has refused, with true courage, to let me change the seating chart. She doesn't want to help me fill the deep void, to help me move on with pointless lesson plans and sucker curriculum. She is a champion of valor. I, on the other hand, pleading with her to reconsider in private, am a pointless model of selfishness.

If you laid eyes on her you would think she was white. She is white. She could change her name to Mary Smith and no one would have any idea she was born and raised in one of the toughest ethnic neighborhoods in Chicago. She's an anomaly in our school. She's white and carries her *mexicanidad* in her surname, Guerrero. No one would think she walks home by herself after midnight from work in an office downtown, through embattled and lonely streets, past vacant storefronts and beat-up cars and gangsters in colors.

On top of the obvious racial distinctions that separate her from her classmates and will, in the coming years, be a striking difference, an odd measuring stick of her success, she is losing her friends left and right to the typical ghetto scenarios we've all heard before. A week before the murder of the Garcia boy, her friend was waiting for her on the stoop in front of Maria's house. The only thing I could get out of Maria was that a car pulled up, asked some questions about the nature of the girl's involvement in the Kings, and then opened fire when they didn't get the answers they were seeking. "They just shot her," Maria had told me. "They shot her on the porch of my house."

Inside the house, Maria's own mother is in the process of erasing herself, killing herself with the hundred-proof dreariness afforded to some welfare mothers and lovers of tough men with macho Mexico in their blood. Maria gets straight A's and her test scores are sky-high despite having a family that's lost its moral ground. Her mother is a late-stage alcoholic. Maria's father is on house arrest for his fifth DUI. Her younger sister is failing out at the local public high school and is in the beginning stages of drug experimentation and sexual discovery, the kind that undoubtedly leads to bloated bellies, welfare checks and banishment from family functions. Her mother is pregnant for the sixth time with another man who will never take part in a family that grows and grows for all the wrong reasons; it's a life stifled by broken promises, alcoholism and cheap love. Her sister and mother's behavior will lead them to the famed world of *sin vergüenza*-ship, where the wrecked ones, the ones without shame, dwell.

Maria, too, was born to a Mexican father and a white mother. I happened to get more of the brown from my father than she did.

One of the challenges I had as a kid was to escape the plunder of my white friends calling me nigger as the sun beat down in August, turning my skin a dark chocolate, a shade my mother's friends all admired as under the sun they turned bright red like lobsters. My biggest challenge was trying to explain away the obvious differences I held, the possible incongruities of past, mixed marriages and ethnic mixing. Maria has it easy. Maria's white. Maria's got a cakewalk. Sometimes, I try to envision a New White Me! while Maria walks the halls of the school and Little Village, as alien as me walking the streets of suburban Cleveland. I'm an oddity and she is, too. We are, Maria and I, what you might call rare breeds, new Americans, people with pasts that do nothing for us.

My biggest genetic legacy may be alcohol. There's drinking everywhere on my father's side: the father, the uncles, the aunts, the cousins, the brothers, and the grandfather who was murdered because of it outside of some bar in a little Mexican village that has gone to hell and been erased from our memories as we now live our lives in the hyphen. I have an alcoholic grandmother and alcoholic great-grandparents on my mother's side. It's an insistent hell. Jazz and drink, and underneath the revelry: suicidal dreams. My great-grandfather locked himself in his garage, turned on the car and let the sweet fumes of his automobile roll into his lungs so he could fall asleep.

In fulfilling my genetic prophecy, my familial obligations, I am a recovering alcoholic, finally escaping, one day at a time, that appetite for drink my family seems to suffer from, the cross they seem willing enough to bear.

At the Garcia boy's funeral I saw Maria in her element. She wasn't smiling as usual, the way she does when she enters my classroom. When she came in the room, there was no sweet face and smile, a pleasant welcome. The dark, deep down murderous rage that all of my students have in them arrived, a rage that will explode with time, given the proper circumstance.

I searched over the heads of the masses huddled up against church railings and pew backs, against stained glass portraits of the Passion, near marble bowls of holy water, the sanctuary slightly smelling of incense. I searched the tired, the poor, sobbing and moving from knees and prayer to feet and song. I searched the church for Maria and instead found the roughest gangbangers around. And behind them and their shaved heads and demonic shags growing out from the back of their scalps, I saw Maria hiding. And, from what I gather, the only thing kids in these situations can gather behind is this: the brute force and pomp of the local gang, in this case the Two Six Nation, the gang the Garcia boy was purportedly involved with.

Maria prayed and sobbed quietly behind them. The girl who raises objections to my theories in class about the nature of the slave narrative in American literature and its obvious influence upon blues music, American politics and American culture; the girl who ferociously defends Gatsby as he dies in a pool, a monster of his own excess, on the grounds that he, although a bit "unsound in his methods," is the symbol of America and its "childlike hope"; the girl who will belittle Fitzgerald as a child for wasting his hopes and dreams in the romantic drivel of alcohol and drugs, sat with the most depraved, most corrupt symbols of modern America and its youth gone awry. There, along with the Holy Ghost and the young shot-up body of her friend, my student, the Garcia boy, in a casket the parents couldn't afford, I knew she plotted out the murder of the killer, only so the cycle could repeat itself, come back around, so the snake can eat its own tail, so we can continue to tell the story we are so attracted to.

Nowhere better than the church to plan a murder, gain stories and perpetuate the ferocity of the America my first-generation students have come to know in a fury of dizzying cynicism.

My mother says my dad wanted to go back to college. "When it came to numbers, he was quite smart. I have never seen anyone use them and be so good with them," she says. "He had scholarships in Mexico to study at the university." I try to picture my father in this world, studying numbers and theory, chalk against blackboard, adding and subtracting equations, rounding up to the nearest 10th. How long would it take if Car X is driving 90 miles an hour to hit that brick wall ahead on the Kennedy Expressway? How long will it take if Man X drinks a lifetime and does cocaine on the side to become a seasoned alcoholic and drug addict?

After the funeral, Maria stood with the gangbangers and looked over the streets waiting for something to happen. While funerals are supposed to be moments free of the violence that caused them, there isn't a better time or place, if you run with the rival gang, to open fire on the whole lot. Everyone is there. Everyone is rangy and terrified. Everyone's packing heat. Everyone's eyes, behind the tears, are edgy, looking for the weakest spots in the perimeter around the small brick church, beyond to the two-family houses and gangways that separate them. If I didn't know her and saw her standing there with those boys, I would have edged away, checked for my wallet. If I was in my car, I would have locked the door, but that could just be the white boy in me.

A playground, around the corner, behind the church, ached in the wind that rolled in, swing sets moved mysteriously, seesaws moaned. The merry-go-round moved slightly, edging toward a rotation.

Maria talked quietly with the *cholos* and one of them put his arm around her and she let him tug her into him. She was tiny in his tattooed arms and massive hands. And then I thought they were just kids, these guys and Maria, comforted only by the fact that they could still touch one another and goddamned thankful they weren't the ones being hustled out the church doors, past priests and onlookers and clumsy pallbearers feeling the weight of not only a real body under the polished mahogany, but the weight of sadness and despair. I wondered if Maria sensed this as she watched the casket rise and fall in the air above the shoulders of the living as they carried it to the limousine, because we had touched on these themes in my class, time and time again. Because this was the real lesson, this was what we could call hands-on learning. I wanted to pull up my lectern and gather my class around me and tell them that despite this death, this pain and misery, there is still that playground and all the creaking and teetering of empty swing sets and this, this is the green light Fitzgerald mused about, and if we can't search out symbols then we don't have the luxury of calling ourselves Americans or aspiring to be American.

On the opposite street corner a bar opened up. Its sign said, in neon, "*Cerveza Fría.*"

Maria wanted to look back and say she did it all by herself. Where she got this type of steadfastness, I didn't know. It was this subversive take on the American maxim of Know-How and Might that would take her away from the mainstream we wanted our kids at the school to take part in, for better or worse. I would never have told her that. I wanted her at Yale. She wanted DePaul.

I pulled Maria aside one day after class. She looked terrible. Her eyes were red and throughout class she had tried her best to keep it all together. As the class left and she hustled her things into her bag, I said, "Maria, do you have a couple of minutes?"

She looked at her friends leaving her one by one, then nodded her head yes.

In the quiet, now empty classroom, in the slight, blue morning light flashing in through the windows, I asked her, "What's wrong?"

"With what?"

"You."

She shook her head and then the tears began. "Nothing."

"Then why are you crying?"

She told me, "Because my mother. My mother is spending all of our money."

Everything spilled out of her. Her books fell to the floor as she dropped down into a seat and her bag fell to her feet. Somewhere out the window a jackhammer drove into the ground. The metallic echo resonated through the room, through the building.

"What do you mean she's spending all of your money?" I asked her.

Through the tears and slight sobs, she told me that her mother drank too much and her father didn't help and then, "We never can pay the bills, the phone, the electric. We never have anywhere to live. We're always moving."

I told her, naively enough, "It'll be okay."

"My brother, he's so little, and sometimes he doesn't get to eat. I work and then spend the money on him because I don't think he is eating enough. We took him to the doctor because he's always sick. He's skinny. Super skinny. I can see his ribs.

"I hate her. I really do."

"No. You don't."

"Yes. Yes, I do. She parties all the time. Jesus, I'm tired.

I want to do homework. I have tests and papers and more tests. I have bus rides and then I cook dinner and then go get cigarettes for my mom. She plays cards. She listens to music. She drinks. I work. I hate her. Do you know what I'm saying?"

"Not really, I guess. No. I want to. I want to understand, to help. I think."

She looked at me blankly. She gathered her things to go. She apologized.

I wanted to say something. I turned around and started to erase the board, my lecture. "You know, I know something about alcoholism. I think you should stop being so helpful.

"I know that sounds weird and maybe a little wrong, but I think if she knows you're going to always do this stuff she'll keep on doing it. Alcoholics are all about themselves, Maria. They are the best kind of charmers. They can charm anybody, and then, when they know they have them, they use it all up, fast."

I put the eraser down. I looked at her across the room. Her hands were on the desk and she was leaning down into it. She was crying. "I know," she said. "I know."

"Stop doing it. Stop being the mom. You're 17. My God, you should be going to parties, doing teenage things."

But as I said this, I realized that despite all her mother's lies and her father's denunciations, Maria didn't hate her parents. In fact, she loved them and wanted to believe in them so much like any teenager. She wanted some common ground, to take part in some ritual that may resemble Happy Family going to the store, Happy Family sending oldest daughter away to college, Happy Family in cars on road trips to places like Disneyland or the Wisconsin Dells singing songs, being a commercial or the perfect family drama, the Mr. and Mrs. Ward Cleavers, the Mr. and Mrs. Cliff Huxtables, and lately, the Mr. and Mrs. George Lopezes.

Maria asked me, "I'm going to be late. Can I get a pass to my next class?"

My father likes to tell stories about the time he crossed the border, which vary from telling to telling. One time while drunk, he told me that when he was 19 years old he found the body of a dead *gringo* in an alley. He told me, "*Mijo*, I found this body and I searched his pockets. His wallet was in the inside pocket of his jacket. I took the money. I took his ID. I went home and put a picture of myself over his face. With his money, I bought a new suit, a *New York Times* and a *Time* magazine at the train station in Juárez. I figured this was what many *gringos* wear and read. I boarded a train and never looked back."

He drank the rest of his beer and, with some effort, reached around to grab another from the cooler on the floor, squeezed a lime into it and sipped it again.

"*Mijo*, I tell you it was great. I rode that train all night and all day past Texas towns, past *La Migra*, past cattle yards, past ranches that looked so much like my father's. Wide awake, I rode in this great suit and saw the whole thing roll out in front of me. I didn't know what was going to happen to me. All I knew was it must be greater where I was going to go than it was where I had been coming from."

And like that, I knew that everything I had ever done had been planned out and spiked into me like a plug in a socket. A jolt. A spark. The whole engine of my life revved up and down to that little mantra I could say to myself over and over again, and my father had probably said to himself driving drunk, working overtime for nothing, marrying a *gringa* and experiencing divorce. He crossed borders. And I was a symbol of that, a living tangible one. I was the most American thing my father knew and I was nothing, a mere phantasm of hope, a wellspring of desire and drama. I was the sum total of America for my father, and this, quite possibly, is why the prodigal son's cross was too much to bear. Not that he inherited possible greatness from his father, but that he became the answer, the end of the equation, the truth of the matter.

I asked Maria, at lunch one day, "Do you have a picture of your father?"

Startled, she told me she did not. She dug through her wallet. She said, "He used to look better. He doesn't look so good now. Anymore."

"Yeah. You should see my dad now."

She nodded, unimpressed, busy searching through her purse, her wallet. I told Maria, "I look at the old pictures of my dad sometimes and laugh. He was such a different person."

I didn't know why I told this to my student, but somehow I knew the embarrassment she felt showing me a picture of a man whom, on some level, she was awfully ashamed of and had nothing more to say to or about.

"Yeah," she said. "He's red."

"What do you mean, red?"

"From the booze," she said, holding up a picture. The man in the picture was my father, I thought. The thick moustache, the bloodshot eyes, glassy and lost. I saw it there, in the shot, taken in what looked like a basement: lousy pictures of old dusty Mexico, a cross and the framed carnival gaudiness, whimsical tackiness of a Virgin Mary behind him on a wall of cheap wood paneling. He stood with his arms crossed over a huge paunch, guarding something mysterious, possibly himself.

My father told me, while drunk, that when he was 19 years old he silently hovered like a hawk watching the way *La Migra* covered the border. "Day and night," he said. "Day and night, *mijo*, I waited with other *Mexicanos* for the perfect moment, the right moment to hop the border, to swim the old river."

He pulled on his beer. He pushed his big hand through his hair, now graying at the temples, making him look wiser than he needed to be or ever was. He was deep into a good drunk and pulling another variation of running the border out from wherever it is that he keeps them.

"*Mijo*, the night we ran I could see the lights of the United States just over the border, on the other side. I was so excited I couldn't stand it. What was waiting for me was something great, something deeply needed, something that had to be done.

"There were six of us. I forget their names, but one of them was a woman and she was pregnant. She said her biggest dream was to have her baby in the United States. She was going to have the baby at any moment. We weren't going to take her, but it was this one guy's wife so we had to. She was a woman, you know."

He fell silent for a moment.

"*Mijo*, I was going to be the first, the first to cross the river, to make a life. I was going to make it and I kept saying this to myself as I swam against the current into Texas with the pregnant woman, her arms around my neck, her husband, that coward, hundreds of yards ahead into the great darkness. She cried on my shoulder and we were wet, heavy with wet. Our clothes, our hair, our arms and legs. We were walking through mud it seemed. She hung on though, her and her unborn baby. They hung on."

The whole shtick is tired, I felt like saying. Get over it, *Dad*, I wanted to tell him as harshly as possible. I wanted to clue him in to how my earliest memories of my mother were waking up late, her leaning over to kiss me, telling me she loved me, smelling like hamburgers and fried chicken because she worked the late shift at the local diner up the block from the apartment we had, telling me she waited tables all night, in and out of dirty stale kitchens wearing cheap sneakers, muddied with grease and lard, the excess of cheap food. She tried all night to make me laugh, herself probably wanting to cry because her feet hurt, her head hurt from the obnoxious remarks of horny, late night diner men, the rank putrid air around the hot grills she slaved over near all night, probably wanting to cry because she still had a couple of hours of studying left for school the next day. I wanted to tell him, as he lied, the truth. I wanted to strangle him with memories.

When I came to from my deep cloud of cynicism, my father was saying, "*Mijo*, that current was strong. That we made it was unbelievable. I thanked God when we reached a part of the river where I could grab onto a stick big enough to pull us into safety. It was then that she started to groan and tell me strange things I couldn't make out above my heavy breathing. Hiding behind some brush, under the stars, she told me she was going to have the baby. I told her, 'No, you can't yet. You must wait.' I told her, 'Wait till we get to a city.' But, no, she was going to have that baby then and there. I was 19, *mijo*, 19 years old. And I delivered a baby on the shores of the Rio Bravo, inside the United States. Boy, did that baby cry. It cried so loud I thought *La Migra* was going to hear us out there in the dark."

My dad stood up, opened the fridge, grabbed another beer and took a drink. He watched and studied me and knew I didn't believe him anymore, the past, the things he told me.

"I mean, look at this," he said, grandly sweeping his hand over the little kitchen he shares with his new wife and kids, the little burned-out kitchen with the worst of tackiness hanging on the walls and crucifix after crucifix and saints and Mexican flags and the blow-to-the-belly smell of fried pork rinds and menudo. "Look at this, *mijo*. I've made it."

I wanted to remind him of that night he and I drove drunk together down the Eisenhower Expressway, him calling my mother a bitch and whore, in English and Spanish, both languages stingingly untrue and me telling him to pull over. "I'll kill you," I said, dirty drunk.

Father and son took swings at one another on the side of a snowy highway, the downtown lights of Chicago behind us, thick snowflakes blowing through the orange lights of the streets in front of the dark, abandoned homes of the South Side, silent, beaten and sodden.

I threw a whopping right hook that landed on the side of his big face. He staggered backward and then looked at me, his hand at his head. He laughed. Then he inched in furiously, his fists up in the air, breathing heavy like a bull. I stood there. Cars whizzed by. Someone honked. The sound of it trailed off into the distance.

He swung, landing a left hook. I felt my nose break, some teeth come loose. I fell to the ground, the snow and ice numbing my hands, sore and swollen. Blood in the snow. He stood over me, said, "Had enough, *mijo?*"

I stood up with his help and then leveled him with a shot to the body and a quick jab to the head, again and again and again. He fell on his ass. Standing over him, laughing, I said, "No. No way. Not nearly enough."

A billboard said, "Miller High Life. The Champagne of Beers." There was music coming from our car, fast, hypnotic Mexican music, too much accordion, too much something. I couldn't tell as my father laid into me and I laid into him. The two of us swapping punches, rights and lefts, hooks and counter-hooks. Blood on our lips, on our knuckles. Mud and dirt on our pants.

The next morning I relayed the fight to my mother, looking for the pity only a mother can give a son, but all she said was, "Maybe you two needed that." Then she laughed, said, "You two need to get over yourselves."

Maria told me her father ran the border. She, too, had the river, the swimming, the wet legs and arms, and nights under the fall of darkness.

My father fled the bullets and the mayhem of a country lost in the wild winds of a dust storm, the ghosts of Pancho Villa nobody cares about anymore, the Emiliano Zapata who failed his people, the Mexico City earthquake and the nightmare hangovers from drinking bathtub tequila or mezcal.

Maria is in the process of applying to Brown after much encouragement and, although the risk is there that she may shrug her teachers and me off, she makes a pretty good show at giving us the best story. She writes in her personal statement, in an essay she calls "Talk is Cheap," "They all expected me to stumble like my father and fall short like my mother. They laid out my life before their eyes: at 17 years old, I would be pregnant with a refrigerator full of beer."

Who "they" is I don't know, but I am fairly sure it is the majority population out there in the America she has yet to engage herself, the "weirdness" of white folk and their culture, even though she herself is the same, the one kid from our school who, whether you want to admit it or not, can make it solely because of her whiteness, her so-called Privilege. Imagine, she'll check a box to identify herself on her college applications. It will be the one that says, "Latino," "Hispanic," "Mexican-American," whatever is the latest way to define us. Imagine when she shows up for an interview. Unlike the Garcia boy, who never made it out of the neighborhood, Maria Guerrero could be headed for Brown.

3

UNIVERSE

It was a 90-minute Memorex cassette tape. It had a pink sticker across the top and was labeled "Family History" in black ink. My Great-Aunt Universe gave it to me to listen to some time ago.

Universe is the matriarch of the Italian side of my family. She owes her unusual first name to her dad's love of the night sky, his deep love for the mystery of space. My great-grandfather, Francesco Torchia—changed to "Frank Torch" on Ellis Island—came over from the Calabria region in Southern Italy, in the first years of the 20th century. After working as a coal miner in West Virginia, he eventually moved with his wife, Daisy, to Perry, Ohio, where he ran a landscaping business. As Frank's oldest child, Universe has played the role of family historian, the keeper of knowledge, the guardian of the joys and tragedies of family life. She is the holder of the Torch family mythology, all the little details and significant moments. She has recorded it all and put it in notebooks. She amassed pictures, kept jewelry, kept dishware, all the things that made up a material life. And, in the process, she collected, quite by accident, the transcendent parts of the lives that had now come and gone. She put it on tape for whoever wanted to listen. Her telling is now more a part of the history of the family than an actual document that maps it out in any objective way. Her chronicle made the story of our lives more complex.

She gave me the tape one day when we met in the Little Italy neighborhood in Cleveland over coffee and pastries. I held the tape in my hand after she handed it to me, listening closely to what she had to say.

"Don't lose it now," she said, taking a bite of her *pasticciotto*, a cream cheese pie that looks rather plain to the sight but when bitten into is rich and flavorful. "If you lose it I don't know what I'd do. I might forget everything. I don't remember things like I used to."

"I won't. I promise. I won't lose anything. It'll be safe and sound." I hefted the weight of the tape in my hand. I stared at it and then put it in my pocket.

She had always been a beautiful older woman. She'd become more regal in these recent years, especially as she had taken it upon herself to be a raconteur of times gone by. She knew that for the members of the Torch family to know anything about ourselves, we might have to go through her. She was a small woman, skinny, and her oversized clothes almost erased her. She wore heavy handmade jewelry she found at local art galleries in Little Italy. Her hair was salt and pepper, which added a weight to her being.

Universe told me she was more Italian now than she ever was growing up, when she was closer to the thing called Italy, when her father and mother spoke Italian in the home and when they had particular cultural customs they followed. Her Italian pride welled up when she talked about her father and mother.

Italy, a country far away from the immediate experience of my family, was very much a part of who they are now as the older generation. When she said "Frank" or "Daisy," one could tell she immediately thought "Italy" or "the Old Country." In her mind, my great-grandparents are the sum total of a country that was across an ocean and long gone, erased the day Frank set foot on the island of Manhattan.

For my Great-Aunt Universe, Italy was a feeling in the heart, an American version of the Italian. It was a wholly American experience, her memory of such a place on a map. It was not the Naples I have roamed, the Rome I have traveled, the Cosenza her father is from, where I have wandered among its strange, crowded buildings. Italy, the very idea of it in my great aunt's head, in my family's collective subconscious, was a shared American phenomenon.

"Everyone hated us," she told me. "No one liked us. We looked different. We smelled different. We got really dark in the summer. We were short and stocky. There was nothing about us that was like anyone we lived around. Everyone was tall and white. Everyone spoke clean English. Good Lord, nobody was even Catholic. It was so hard on us kids. We were always trying to get away from it, to get past being Italian." She looked out the window, at the passing cars, the people walking by. The reflection of the sun came through the glass and spilled out into a rainbow across the floor, having been refracted into a million rays of light. She told me, almost offhandedly, tracing the past all the way up to the present moment, "Now we're white. We're just white." The way she said it was like a condemnation; she was indicting a whole family's choices and actions. "All of us," she said, looking at me, "we're just white. I guess we're just American."

After we finished our coffee, I helped her back to her car. We walked along in silence, letting dusk take hold. The sun hung low in the horizon over the brick streets and old two-story duplex homes. As we walked through a Little Italy that wasn't so Italian anymore, we heard Dean Martin over the speakers outside an antique store singing "That's Amore." Statues of Christopher Columbus guarded the front door of a grade school that was dedicated to the memory of him.

The smell of homemade pizza flowed out from kitchens and into the street. My aunt walked with her arm through mine. She was a fragile woman, and I wondered why I had never paid attention to her, the power of her and her sway over our familial history. I looked down at her and she looked up at me.

She said, "You know, Raffi, you're so handsome. You're such a good boy. Just so handsome." She patted my arm and I laughed. She said, "Don't laugh. You are. You look like your father. Your mother is a good-looking gal, but your father, he was a real looker."

I said, "When was the last time you saw my dad, Aunt Universe?"

"Why? Does it matter? People don't change. That young man was just so sweet and just so good-looking. We all thought so. Your mother was a very lucky woman." She winked. "He was quiet, but he had such a large presence." She went silent, and then, "Don't you laugh at me because you think I can't remember. I remember everything, Raffi." She stopped in her tracks. We stopped. She took her arm from mine and said, "I might be old but I remember. You're a Torch for sure, but, boy, you look like that father of yours. What was his family name?"

"Garcia."

"Garcia. Yes. That's it. You have a lot of Garcia in you. It's clear."

We continued walking.

"Do you doubt me? You wouldn't doubt an old lady, would you?"

"No, ma'am."

"Oh. Now you're just placating an old lady."

"No, ma'am."

She laughed and grabbed my arm again. When we reached her car, she rolled down the window and looked up at me. She touched my cheek as I bent down to say goodbye to her. She told me, "Now, Raffi, don't be such a stranger."

She had always said my name like this. Although she knew full well that I preferred the nickname "Rafa," I had always been "Raffi" to her. No matter how many times I told her that she was taking liberties with my name, she still called me "Raffi."

"You should see me more often," she added. "I mean it. You're like a stranger."

"I live in Chicago, Universe."

"So what? You can't make time for an old lady? I could die soon."

"You aren't going to die, Aunt Universe. Not tomorrow."

"Maybe not tomorrow, Raffi. But I am going to die. It is the surest, most truthful thing I have ever said."

"Yes."

"Okay. Listen to me. You don't lose that tape. You're in charge of it."

"I know," I told her. I patted my jeans pocket.

"Be careful and be good."

"I will. Buckle up, Aunt Universe."

The sky was turning a dark purple at the edges. She'd be lucky to get on the highway before dark, back to the west side of Cleveland, where she lives by herself now, her husband having died many years ago and her kids long gone, one dead.

She put her foot down on the accelerator and drove slowly over the brick streets of Little Italy. As I watched her, she waved at me, her hand out the window. I put my hand in my pocket, grabbed the tape, smiled and waved back at her.

Universe was saying, "Testing." She spoke into the microphone—almost too close, as the sound was rough and grainy. She said, "This is a test." There was a ruffling of papers in the background, and then, "I don't know if this will answer your questions, but here goes. I don't even know if any of this is right, but I'll tell you everything I know. We always need to know and remember where we're from, so here you go. It's as good as it gets, this tape and these memories."

She was speaking to someone else. The tape was made in 1992, when I was only 17. I was drinking an incredible amount of alcohol by then and beginning to experiment with drugs. I was too far into the very serious business of erasing myself to be interested in a narration or a reconstruction of the history of my family. I couldn't remember the previous day, let alone try to mine a collective memory. In many ways I was unprepared to head down that path and dig out the recollections that have shaped my American family.

"I'd figured I'd make this for my kids, and when I did, at least they'll know me. They will know where we all come from because, well, it is important to know where we all come from.

"More than that, it is important that one knows the truth about where they come from," Universe said. "Young people only care about the houses they live in and the cars they drive and all that kind of stuff. Little do they know that the choices and actions they make have been in the making for a long time, before they were even born. Maybe no one will listen to me. I don't know.

"Maybe no one cares. Maybe people think this whole thing is like Narcissus looking into the pond at his own reflection. But I don't care. Then look into the reflection I will."

I was sitting in my mother's car after Universe pulled away, listening to the tape she gave me. I rolled down the window and leaned back. Even though I had just seen her and had a conversation about the tape with her, there was an unsettling eeriness to the voice. Maybe it was the age of the tape, the graininess that made her voice rough and strange.

Two men were sitting on the porch across the street from where I was sitting. They stared at me as I listened. I put my hand up in greeting and they ignored me, going back to drinking coffee and playing cards.

Why did my great-grandfather leave Italy? What goes into leaving the place of origin other than the need to find a better life? It must be more than this, some other kind of complex system of belief or faith in some strange myth. In the communal family memory I have to tap, I am only aware that, "Italy was hard." I hear, "He was poor." I listen to, "Frank wanted to find a wife." My usual retort—"Is this enough to leave your homeland, alone, at 21?"—is always returned with a casual shrug, and sometimes, "Does it have to be anything else? What else is there? Why not?" Did poverty and hard times reach the point where Frank just got up and left one day, saying to himself, "I am leaving"?

My mother's family, safeguarded by 96 years of American self-assurance, struggles to come to terms with the reasons. We are left with the terminal residue of a man, his vision for himself and his life—an illustration and caricature of all the reasons for leaving his homeland. In the early 21st century, cushioned by an age defined by doing whatever gets you off, Frank Torch becomes a stereotype of the European immigrant. It's as if by coming to the United States—for very valid reasons, I'm sure—to become someone somewhere, he became, rather, an anyone anywhere, a person devoid of any tangible human qualities.

On the Memorex tape, Universe said, "Ellis Island." Her voice, far away and dreamy, like the whistling of the wind on a winter day, said, "New York City got to be too big for him. You know, he was just a small town guy. I mean, he came from such a small place back in Italy. He was so poor. Everyone was so poor. He must have tried to find his way there, working odd jobs and stuff like that. Thinking back, I can't help but feel so sorry for him. I can just picture Dad wandering around aimlessly. I suppose some of this wandering aimlessly could be me not knowing enough about who he is. But wander he did, I am almost sure of it. God, he used to hate big cities. Even when we lived in Perry and we'd have to go into Cleveland for something he would hurl nasty words at the city.

"Anyway, he ultimately made his way to Grafton, West Virginia. There, he got on with a mining company as coal miner and…I don't remember everything my father told me. I can only picture what it must have been like. What a horrible place it must have been. My father never talked about it. It was like he fought a war or something because those times were just left unspoken. West Virginia, those coal mines, were something us kids thought about in our imaginations, if we thought about it all. All at once, they were the very thing that made my father who he was, shaped his American experience, and also they were taboo. His history became a mania almost, something I have always thought about. I can't say for sure. I don't even remember how I know all this stuff, where I got it. Dear Lord, I don't even know how any of this has even gotten into my head."

Not too long ago, I had dinner with Aunt Universe's brother, my grandfather Carl. We were at TGI Fridays—not far from the place where I grew up—sitting around a table with my mom and one of my uncles. I had been asking my mom a lot about the origins of the Torch family here in Ohio. I wondered for a long time why Frank would bring them here of all places. As we were waiting to order our food, I asked my grandfather, "Why did Frank come to the United States?"

My grandfather mulled it over. An Ohioan through and through, he's not a man who had advanced ideas that were more complex than necessary. "I don't know. To be honest, I haven't thought about it. We were from here and that was that. Growing up I didn't have a whole lot of time to think about these things, Raf. I didn't have the luxury." He looked at me and smiled. "We had a Depression. We fought in wars. Who the hell cared where my father was from or any father, for that matter?"

I laughed and held my hands up like he was robbing me at gunpoint. "Okay. Fair enough."

My mother jumped in. "Dad, seriously. Answer the question. There must have been a reason. He was your dad. You must know."

"Tari, we didn't think about these things," he said. "I don't even remember being a child sometimes. Give me a break. I'm an old man. Thinking hard makes me tired."

He looked around for the waitress.

Aunt Universe told my family through the tape, "It was my father's silence that shaped me more than the things he ever said to me. I wanted him to talk always and always, and then, deep inside, there was my esteem for his silence, a thing I wanted to handle like an ornament or tool. I wanted to hear and not hear. Does that make sense? I don't know what I am saying. Hopefully this translates. Now, thinking back, this is what I inherited. This is being a Torch.

"All of us were interested in hearing about where he came from. Sometimes he would come out and tell us stories about that time, but most of the time we had to prod him to tell us anything at all. His presence would spark within me a need to know more about him even if I thought I knew all I could know. His stories never slaked my need to know him. I remember every detail of the past he deemed important enough to share. His stories freed me from my own imagination and the fictions that could come from it. My father was always a thing too big for me to manage alone. I found that I was making things up to fill out the space he found he didn't need to fill up. I felt dangerous, like I had stabbed him in the back or something. It was the strangest feeling, like I had done more to him than he had done to himself.

"He never did tell us how he got that nasty scar near the top of his leg, near his hip. It was something he never talked about. Most of the men I knew from my father's generation had these moments, these kinds of wounds. They had a ton of emptiness that we all just had to fill in if we wanted to know anything about where we came from or who we were, if it is true that we inherit the pasts of those that come before us. But what does it mean if I make things up? What kind of history have I been given if it is one that I have made up in the process of hearing bits and scraps or nothing at all? Where do I come from? Who am I? I am Universe. But, really, who am I?"

4

SUMMER 2003

It's been four months since the Garcia boy died, and I'm writing all of this in the dark. Long shadows fall across the floor of my bedroom, the extra room my mother and my stepfather, Tom, have set aside for me when I visit them in Cleveland. I am alone and the city hums in the distance. No cars pass by in the street. All seems desolate and lost. It is a blank, still night, hot and sticky, and the windows are wide-open. I am bare-chested and sweating. A drowsy breeze comes in, whipping up the curtains, but not enough to make the heat any easier to take. The ambiance is not necessarily unpleasant, but rather a constant reminder of why I'm here at home again. My mother's had a heart attack, and she almost died. The medical term for heart attack is myocardial infarction. I write this phrase six times in a row in the left-hand margins of the paper.

My mother almost died on the operating table. They had opened her up to do their work, and she died; but then they saved her after a few tense moments. The doctors told me this when I came into town. Tom told me too. He is a tough guy, an Irish-American recovering alcoholic. He told me he screamed her name when he was alone, and that haunts me.

I Google "heart attack" and in one-tenth of a second 48,100,000 websites turn up. I click on one at random and find out that a heart attack occurs when the blood supply to part of the heart muscle, the myocardium, is severely reduced or stopped.

My mother told me that she was starting to believe my history. She told me this the other day as she was in recovery. She said, "Rafa, it's amazing. I think I believe you." She wanted stuff to read while she was stuck there in the hospital, and so I gave her some chapters to read. I told her it's a book about our family— well, my family, the Mexican side and the Italian. My mom wanted me to tell other stories, stories that aren't in the book, like my maternal grandmother, Sondra's.

"There's just not enough room," I said.

"You mean some people make it and some don't?" she asked me, eating ice chips I'd gotten for her from the nurses' station.

I shrugged. "Yeah. That's always how it works when people write history."

"Who chooses?"

"I do. The writer," I told her, looking at the cards people had sent her since her arrival.

"Based on what?"

She smiled a little, but I could tell she was upset that I was telling some events and not others. My mother had always been big on telling the whole story in some traditional way she couldn't define but knew about and clearly felt that I wasn't tuned into. She probably thought it's kind of a lie if I didn't tell every-thing. She believed in the whole truth.

"Good stories," I said. I laughed. I sounded a little heartless.

"There're good stories on Grandma's side, Rafa."

"Mom, let's face it, the Hamiltons were Waspy. They were wealthy and alcoholic, which is interesting in an F. Scott Fitzgerald story maybe, but it's just not new. To be honest the only real interesting story is your grandfather killing himself."

"Rafael!" she yelled. She grew tight-lipped, and then said, in a whisper, "Yeah, you're right." She chuckled.

"It's exciting stuff. Guy, depressed, writes a letter to his wife, leaves it on the counter in his nice kitchen, gets in his car, turns it on and waits for sleep. Good stuff. That kind of material never gets old."

I was pushing the envelope a little, and my mom stopped me. She said, "That's sick. You're sick."

"Thanks." After some time, I asked, "Do you need anything else?" I held her hand.

"No. I just thank you for coming. You shouldn't have."

"That's a ridiculous thing to say, Mom. Don't say that. You had a heart attack. You—"

I almost told her that she nearly died, but I didn't. We sat silently for a while. There was a huge wound on her chest that I didn't want to look at, so I tried not to. We talked about other things for some time, and then she said, "It's just sad."

"What's sad?"

"Our story. Ours. I guess the whole act of reading it makes me need to believe it. When it's on paper, it sounds so sad. Why does reading it make it seem true and sad?"

"Because it is. You should believe it," I told her. "Anyway, maybe the story could move us forward. I don't know."

"Are we stuck?"

"No. Yes. I don't know. Maybe not stuck, but doesn't it make you hopeful?"

"In a way."

"What way?" I asked.

She said, "That we have moved forward. I just don't see it the same way as you. I think I would write something different. Something true." I rolled my eyes. She smiled. I told her, "I guess I don't know where it's supposed to go."

I held her hand and it looked old. When did that happen? When I was little I used to be in love with her hands because they were beautiful and strong, yet delicate and always manicured. Now they were white and pale and bloated, slightly yellow. Now there were tubes in her arms. She was hooked up to machines. Some unnatural sound came from her lungs when she took in oxygen and let it go.

"You'll figure it out. But I believe you. Even if you are making things up, even if you exaggerate," she told me, smiling.

"Jesus, Mom. I'm not making things up."

"It's okay," she said, patting my hand. "Take us forward. It's okay."

When I heard the news about my mom, I was with some of my students in Colorado. I was in the wilderness. We were going to climb to the top of a mountain near a town called Eagle. Lauren, a fellow literature teacher, and I were in charge of seven kids. We were participating in a program where they take inner-city kids and put them into the wild. It was an intense experience. Everyone carried what was necessary: a pack filled with food, one or two pairs of underwear, a flashlight, a change of clothes, one pair of socks. No soap and no toothbrush. No makeup or blow-dryers. One roll of toilet paper for each person. One of the kids carried the shit shovel. We had to dig a hole, shit in it, and then cover it up or put it in a bag and take it back down the hill with us. Our own shit.

On the first day, I drove us out of Chicago. We were all in a rented 15-passenger van. We drove through parts of the country that none of the kids had ever seen or even imagined, their parents mostly immigrants, never leaving Chicago for any reason. Lauren and I talked for a while after we left Chicago until we entered Iowa. Then the conversation stalled as we became more aware of the kind of mileage we were going to have to do to get to Colorado. What could we possibly talk about in this marathon? Sometimes she drove and sometimes I did. The kids got rowdy, but nothing terrible. Normal kid stuff, like screaming and laughing and the occasional crude joke that I pretended not to hear because they were on summer vacation and I didn't want to be the dean anymore. I was just there to drive and watch them climb a mountain.

On the first night, we stayed at a campsite that Lauren and I picked out because it had a pool and an open pit for barbecue. The kids immediately changed clothes, dove in and yelled, "Mr. Torch, ain't you getting wet? Jump in!"

The water looked so crisp and cool. I took off my shirt and jumped in. We all threw around a football and told each other stories. They mostly told me stories about themselves, and I listened as best as I could because they rambled on, moving from memory to memory without any order. They moved from one relative to another, from Mexico to the United States and back again. They brought us through various place and times—even if they didn't know them personally—because these places and times were mostly the accumulation of their parents' experience in the United States, a beleaguered, hallucinatory experience from what I gathered.

Eagerly, they told me everything they knew, even if I doubted the veracity of it. Then I would tell them little stories about myself and they listened intently because, well, I was their dean, and they thought I spent all my time at the school. They thought that I was this guy who loved giving detentions and had no youth, that somehow I came from nothing, was a man from nowhere, dropped into their lives to make them miserable. When I told them some of the things I used to do as a kid—fail classes, cut school, sneak out of the house late at night—they laughed. We were building something that day in the pool.

The sun pulverized us even as it was setting off in the horizon over the tree line. We got hungry under the weight of it all, the sun, the remembrance, the knowledge that we still had so far to go. I drove to the store, picked up some hot dogs and hamburger meat and chips and grape soda. When I got back to the site, we cooked it all up and gorged ourselves, set up our tents, told more stories. The kids were very good storytellers. Their lives reminded me of my own, even though they came from different places. Somewhere deep inside, I couldn't help but be moved by their narratives. There was a river running behind us and strange noises came from it all night long. It wasn't really a river. It was more of a creek. White, milky water ran in it like the riverbed was made of clay. Big gnarly trees made a canopy over our heads. We were sheltered and felt safe for the time being all the way out here in the nothing of America.

After a while, the kids started to wander off around the campsite. There were only two boys; the other six kids were girls. You could feel the tension, at least with the boys. I had to share their tent. I felt sorry for them. The boys were always trying to be cool and heavy and scrappy. One of them was named Felipe and the other was named Ricardo. Felipe was heavy-duty. He was so excited about getting to the top of that mountain. Ricardo was, too, but it was different for him. He was older by a year. Felipe was aching to get there. Ricardo was much more patient. He could see it, smell it, hear it calling him, but he was patient and he would be the leader after I left them. It was something heavier for him in a transcendent way. He wouldn't be able to tell me that if I had asked him, but I knew it just by looking into his eyes. He had a faraway look that made me ache with the desire to be young like him again and be able to see such things for the first time.

For Ricardo, the mountain was just another dilemma to conquer, a problem to be solved with the spirit and will. Felipe was dreamy. He was all muscle and passion. Felipe wanted to conquer the physicality of it. He wanted to feel the rocks and the cold-water streams, and breathe in the thin air and clench his fists and tighten his muscles at the top of the world.

The two of them stayed up all night talking to each other. They told each other things in half whispers. Their stories dared one another to top the other. The bulk of their tales were filled with a heartache and sadness that they laughed at occasionally. I feigned sleep and listened to all the things they said.

Ricardo told Felipe about his mother and how he hated her and wanted to move out of the house, but he always had to take care of his brothers and sisters even though he said he loved them more than anything else in life. Felipe told him how he hated living with his grandmother, how he wished he could see his dad, who was a long-distance trucker, more and that he liked the woman his dad had married after his mom.

Felipe told Ricardo that his father hit him sometimes but that's because he was "teaching me a lesson whenever I needed to learn something new." You didn't hear a word of dissent from Ricardo. I think Ricardo knew about that stuff, too. I thought to myself, "I can relate." I wanted to ask the kid, "How do you tell everything? What's important and what's not, and how do you say things without asking or seemingly asking for pity?" I wanted to open up my eyes and look them in the face and tell them about all those years I drank and hated my father, but "it wasn't really hate," I would say, because I don't know if it was. "I think I was confused and eager to lay blame and point fingers."

I would ask them, "What's important? What's at stake? What's the heart of the matter of our lives? Tell me something about my life," I would beg them. And they would turn to me and say, "We already have."

My mother told me about anything other than the way she felt, which was okay, I thought, because I didn't know if I wanted to hear the truth. I didn't know if I wanted to hear her say, "I'm scared, Rafa." I didn't know if I could help her, and I thought that if she were to tell me about her fear it would imply the need for help from me. I was scared about helping her. I didn't even know how I would go about doing it. In my heart, I knew she needed the help, she needed to feel less afraid. In my heart, I knew.

I tried to make her laugh as often as possible because she seemed to be herself again when she laughed. I told her stories and exaggerated, acting some of them out in front of her bed, much to her delight. She told me, "Rafa, you should be a comedian." She was trying not to laugh because of the pain. She held onto her chest, under her hand a long, strange scar where they tore her open to repair the essential part of her, the thing that would allow her to go on.

"Really," she went on. "You should be a comedian. Your stories are so funny."

The woman in the bed next to my mom was dying. She was very old. I could smell her and her death. Walking by her bed every time I went into the hospital room to see my mother, I was struck by the effort at which I tried not to look at her, at the suffering. Her television was always on. I wondered if she could hear us telling stories, if she believed them because some of them were pretty tall and foolish. She always seemed to be watching *Wheel of Fortune*. Pat Sajak was calling out the letters.

Vanna White was turning vowels and consonants. Someone said, "I'd like to guess the puzzle, Pat."

When we passed into the state of Colorado, the landscape became rolling hills and harsh, burnt-up grass. Everything was yellow and sick. We were all alone on the highway and there were rotten, broken-down fences lining the road. My students slept most of the time in the back of the van. We slowly moved into higher altitudes and our lungs and heads were affected as the oxygen we breathed became thinner and harder to take in. We felt breathless in the heights.

We pulled over at a rest stop to stretch our legs and arms, to walk off the tired that had gripped us for hundreds of miles. Rain came out of the heavens, and for the next few hours, as we went in and out of canyons and the landscape changed in dramatic ways, the kids rode along in the back seat, silent except for the whispers of amazement at the things they were seeing take shape outside the window. They were rejuvenated in the promise of the terrain, the tall cliffs, dense forests and cold-water rivers running alongside us. We were on the edge of arrival.

Before we could climb to the summit we needed to be able to trust one another, to hear when someone needed our help, hear the right words that would signal us to move into action. Trained professionals were there to help us learn these new tactics. They had games and obstacle courses we had to run to train us for the hard times that would baffle us. Mostly it was an exercise in the proper way to speak to one another, what to say and when.

I was not afraid of the heights and the things we'd find up there in the thin air. No, I was afraid of the games that would alter the way we saw and interpreted the world. I was most afraid of the alteration of our stories and the ways we would interact thereafter. While it helped us in our journey, I was most comfortable with the way I had come to know. I did not want to learn another way. I was stubborn, like my father. I pressed into the accelerator and Lauren said, as we raced around the tough curves, moving higher and higher, "Go easy on the speed, will you? You're making me nervous."

My mother didn't want to tell me about her heart attack at first because she thought I should go on this trip into the wild with the kids. Tom took her to the hospital, and the doctors felt it necessary to have major surgery to correct the four clogged arteries that were causing her the shortness of breath that, if untreated, would ultimately lead to her death.

At the end of my long day of learning to trust people and teaching them to do likewise with me, Tom called me on my cellphone to tell me about the heart attack. After we had portioned out all that we'd carry on our backs for the duration of the trip, my stepfather told me, "Rafa, listen. Don't get upset. She's fine." He never wanted me to worry about my mother. He knew that we were very close and he never got in the way of it, despite the almost 20 years of marriage they shared. His own mother had died when he was very young, and he knew the pain and suffering I would endure if my mom was lost. He treaded lightly through the story he had to tell me.

"Your mother. She had a heart attack." I was silent on the other end. He seemed to sense my fear. He said, "She is going into surgery in a few minutes. She'll be fine. In many ways, it's routine."

"I'm coming home."

"You don't have to. Everything's covered. She wouldn't want you to come home."

"That's too bad. I'm getting a flight."

There was silence on both ends. I was in the van parked outside the campground. The afternoon rain was coming down in sheets. Thunder rolled off the cliffs and rock ledges way high up against the sky. I couldn't see through the windshield; the rain was coming down that hard. I could only see the vague outlines of the heights we were going to travel tomorrow at dawn. The rain made things blurry. I was numb. I told Tom, "I'm coming home. I'll call you when I get a flight out of here."

"All right. Be careful. There's no rush, though. She'll be in surgery for hours. It's a long procedure."

"Tell Mom I love her."

"I don't have to. She already knows."

I walked slowly through the rain and opened the door to the room where the kids were packing their goods. Lauren saw me soaking wet, standing stunned in the doorway.

"I'm sorry," I said. "I have to go."

It was then that I realized how far away I was from everything. We were in the valley of three huge mountains, and the road out of here, to Denver, was three hours long. I was worried about getting out of the wilderness.

After dinner we told the kids that I would be leaving them. Ricardo and Felipe, while being empathetic, were wary of me. But if they sensed my fear, they didn't let on. They didn't like fear in adult men; it made them uncomfortable. The men in their lives had masked their fear and inadequacies. They felt they needed to do the same. They watched me and stayed out at the margins, taking me in, seeing how I reacted from moment to moment.

Before lights out, when I'd try to get some sleep before the long ride into Denver at dawn, we gathered together for one last group picture. We smiled as the flash blinded us. We all moaned in our blindness.

In the wee hours of the morning, I got up, showered and waited for my ride. I waited in the dark with my things. I couldn't see 100 yards in front of me. The stars in the sky were brilliant and falling to only God knows where.

Later, during the flight, I thought about just how alone my mother and I were when I was growing up. I had nobody else, and what made me most sad in that cross-country flight was that she really had no one either. My father had gone away to live his own life, to fulfill his own destiny, make his own story matter in the long story he was trying to uphold and live by as if it were a creed, the stories we inherit.

I was most afraid, of all things in my life, of losing my mother because she was the one who informed me about the person I was. The stories she told let us both into our family, even when we felt most alone and at odds with the very things that made us Torches. More than that, my mother informed me, more than my father ever did, about being a Garcia. If my mother died, who would fill me up, make me be?

Suddenly, I was tempted to order a scotch on the rocks and show up shitfaced and belligerent. I could picture it. I would stroll in hours late, drunk and falling around. I'd be arrogant through the corridors of emergency rooms and waiting rooms, luggage in hand, dirty from the mountains, reeking of the wild west and scotch on my lips, sour in my mouth, hitting on nurses and yelling, "Where's my mother? Where's the old lady? Where do they keep the heart patients?" I could drink if I wanted to. If my mother was going to die, why the fuck not?

But instead of that scotch, I drank my club soda and stared out the window of the plane into the abyss below as the captain told us we would be starting our descent into Cleveland Hopkins. As we landed and came smoothly into the gate, I thought about how those kids back in Colorado were in the heights and starting that long and arduous first trek of their journey. They were going up a mountain all excited and guiltless and surprised by the beauty around them. They were just starting out as I was taking my bags down from the overhead compartment and walking up the sloped hallway that connected the airplane with the terminal. Their packs didn't weigh them down yet. Give it time, I said to myself. Let them gather up the miles and sleep in the cold. Let them hear the howl of wolves in the night. Let them, I said. Let them.

I have been here a week now. I have to go back to Chicago, the city of my birth. It's so hot right now and I am sweating and bare-chested and just getting through the fear of losing my mother, but nothing is working. What if you lose the essential element of the story, the truth?

I talked to Lauren today. The kids got back from Colorado. I asked about Felipe and Ricardo, and she told me that they led everyone up that mountain.

"When we got tired, they carried us. Ricardo's patience and Felipe's zeal. It was amazing. Felipe, the higher we climbed, kept yelling out into the horizon. He wasn't screaming anything real or anything you could understand. It was just a yell. A huge yell from the pits of him, and everyone laughed. He did it whenever he saw something beautiful. He did it a lot."

I was jealous not to have been able to see or hear the yell.

"How was the weather?" I asked.

"It was okay. Cold. And then one night, all hell broke loose over us."

"What do you mean?"

"Well," Lauren said, "it rained for a whole day straight and then that night it just began to hail. Everyone was wet and miserable.

Then this intense lightning storm hit us. We were about a thousand yards from the summit and in the wide open. The guides told us we needed to get into the lightning position."

"The what?"

"The lightning position. After you left they told us that if a storm happens, we would have to get into this position, which was like getting into a catcher's position, but with your head between your knees as far as you can go. We had to get as close to the ground as possible without lying down. It was fucking scary. Lightning was smashing down around us. The tents were blowing away. Some of the kids were moaning. Some were outright crying. I'd never seen anything like it before.

"We never did get to the top of the summit. The weather didn't allow it. It was too foggy and the guides wouldn't let us go. We did all that work almost for nothing."

They were so close. They were there and the lightning broke above their heads, and my mother is almost dying tonight and they were almost there, so close. They could see it, the top, the edge, the precipice. On the other side, who knew? They didn't get the chance to see it. But I picture Felipe up there yelling. I picture Ricardo up there, silent and mindful, staring out over the mountaintops like Zarathustra, like a world-weary vet, his headband on and his pack tight on his back, carrying the camp's heaviest load because he's earned it with might and muscle and fortitude.

Tomorrow, I have to go back to Chicago. I can't sleep and it's hot and I'm afraid my mother will die as she sits in her hospital room. I write, "Please help her" in the margins of the page I'm working on.

5

TURBULENCE AND LUMINOSITY

1972/2004

Struck by turbulence, the plane rumbled over the raw landscape below. Outside the little window, there was the vast chaparral of ocotillo, saguaro bushes and desert hills sparsely covered with the burned-out grass of northern Mexico. The clouds ahead were skulking across the valley. Out in the distance, they were building against the ominous blue mountains, *Cerro de la Silla, del Topo Chico, de las Mitras* and *La Huasteca*, like it said in my trusty travel guide that explained all the geographical details and vast historical significance of Monterrey. Here I was, a tourist, in the land of my father.

So much of the place was built up in my mind by the images and visions my parents had shot me up with over my lifetime. My father's: a place of impossibility yet so rich in childhood drama that it has become both a place to repress and desire. My mother's: a place of violence and senselessness, not because of a particular vehemence against Mexicans, but through witnessing the strange, twisted simulacrum the men in her life had become, one by one, each of them succumbing to drink and nightmare.

I had come prepared. I had a Visa card, vague, desultory maps and internet itineraries. Totally ready, I felt the plane gently touch the earth. The flaps on the wings went up, and we slowed to a stop far from any airport gate. The seat belt signs went off and the captain said, "Welcome to Monterrey, *México. Bienvenidos.*"

Once out of the plane, I walked across the tarmac toward a white building that was under construction. The heat struck me hard and unapologetically. Sweat beaded on my skin, ran down my forehead, made my hands sticky. The weight of my belongings was heavy on my back. I looked for a downtown, a cityscape, tall buildings, something familiar and readily readable, but only caught glimpses of low cropped hills and the high jagged peaks of mountains in the distance, slanted by the wavy heat lines in the air far away that made everything seem illusory. I looked over to the west, past the airport landing strip, past the wild valley that gained in elevation. For many years, I had wondered what it would be like to go to this place, to that town; to take my father's journey in reverse, the son going "home." I took in the sights and the smells of the frontier. There was nothing particularly Mexican about the place, other than the writing on the walls near slouched brick buildings and across the billboards out near the highway.

Behind me, they had begun to refuel the plane for the trip back over the border to *Los Estados Unidos.* Ahead of me, somewhere in the labyrinth of hallways and breathless rooms, was Mexican Customs. In my hand I carried my birth certificate, which told them I was a full-fledged citizen of the United States. In my head I carried the rudiments of my father's language. I recited, under my breath and vaguely ashamed, a bare-bones dialogue between me and the Customs agent who was ahead checking bags and documents. I was thinking in English and whispering in a strange, almost illiterate Spanish.

When I reached the agent's desk I said, "*Hola.*" I smiled wide.

"*Su pasaporte. Negocios o vacaciones?*" he asked. He didn't even look at me. He was arranging some papers on his desk. When I didn't answer him, trying to figure out what he said, slowing the language down in my head—translating Spanish into English, getting caught on the "*negocios*"—he looked up at me. He repeated himself. "*Su pasaporte. Negocios o vacaciones?*" He asked slower, drawing out the words, enunciating every word.

"*Yo tengo un certificado de nacio. No pasaporte,*" I told him. I said, "I'm on vacation. A tourist." I pointed at myself, said, "*Turista.*"

The air-conditioning hummed. A long white hallway lay ahead of me, past the entrance gates. It was empty and freshly painted. A sign said, "*Pintura Fresca.*"

The agent stared at me. Then he said, "*Sí. Bueno.*" He snorted and took my papers. He examined them and then stood to check my bags. Occasionally, he looked at me, sizing me up.

Almost whispering, I asked him, waiting for the whole process to end with a group of American businessmen behind me, "*Mi español is muy mal. Habla inglés?*"

"Yeah," he said. "I speak English." He zipped up my bags and handed me my birth certificate. "Now, *pásale, amigo.*" He waved me by, through the gates, into Mexico.

Jimmy Barajas paces from one end of his room to the other all night, every night, his mother told me in a conference. She was worried about his mental state. "Something has changed, Señor Torch," she said in my office after I called her in to talk about Jimmy's performance in class, which had slipped a little. "He tells me he's studying and I believe him. But what young man studies all night long? I hear him. Back and forth. Back and forth. He is suffering."

My student, Jimmy, was searching for something he couldn't articulate. But the problem, I guessed, was right there under his nose. In many ways, it was his neighborhood that plagued him, for if he left it, he felt like he would betray it somehow, and if he stayed, he felt like he would forever hate it for keeping him there.

Leaving the neighborhood for college, as he would have to, was the scariest thing imaginable for the kid. College, the idea of going away, was another land to explore, and somewhere deep inside himself, Jimmy didn't think he was cut out for the whole thing, going to college, living in a dorm, meeting new people—radically different people from radically different places, where their friends weren't murdered in the street, where grandmothers didn't slave for hours making tamales for the holidays and where everyone didn't sound as if they were rumbling over potholes when they spoke English. Jimmy didn't think he was cut out for crossing borders and leaving home. Yet, at the same exact time, he felt like he wasn't cut out for staying put either.

In college I used to wonder what it would be like to go to Mexico, maybe like other Mexican-American kids who've never been down south, home to many of our parents, our relatives. I think sometimes the romanticization of such a place is a part of growing up for us sons and daughters of immigrants, searching endlessly for a home, a hearth, a national space.

At Antioch College, I was in UNIDAD!, the Latino group on campus. For the Chicano students in that group, Mexico was a place way beyond our imagination, a place to retire to, a place to find ourselves. I think over the years I've grown cynical about all those dreams. I think belonging to a group like that made me feel not-Mexican-enough, and isn't that weird? Who is Mexican or American or Italian enough, and if they are not, what does that mean?

Why did I come to this realization there, in Monterrey? What is it about Mexico that makes me reject it? Maybe the answer is in me and always has been and I'm just too frightened to look. Not being Mexican scares me. Not being American scares me. Being Brown and being White scares me. My mother told me that's exactly why I needed to take this trip.

"You can't run from it," she told me before I left. "It's the thing you need to figure out."

My mother has always blamed herself for the angst I feel about my father and Mexico. When I was younger, I tried to steer the conversation away from my father when my mother tried to talk about him. I'd get mad and argumentative and tell her to stop talking about it. It wasn't that I thought of Mexico as a wicked place, but because I equated the country with my father and uncles, the place seemed brutal.

I told my mother, "I don't know what I'm supposed to do down there."

"Do what people do when they go to a foreign country. Walk through the cities, take in the sights, take pictures, visit a museum. Rafa, go and have fun. You're forgetting fun."

I think my mother always saw the relationship I had with my father—or the lack of one—as something easily fixed. He loved me, she would say, and I should love him back. Her narrative was easily mended. It was classical cinema in a way, very American. Everything worked out in the end. The narrative as I saw it was much more complex and troubling. My father's life was problematic. Being a son to a Garcia was something mysterious. It wasn't always clear what my father's narrative wanted of me. I'm not even sure my father knew what his story wanted from him.

While we had names to define us as people in a clan, the very idea of names became irrelevant and senseless. To me, going to Mexico meant going to find out what my name meant, the name that was taken from me when my mother filed for divorce. While

I was no longer a Garcia, I wondered about the presence of it in me. Mexico was the mystery of Being a Garcia.

I sat out in the plaza that first night after the rain fell, washing away the heat. There was a dance in the city center, in the middle of the park, and I watched and listened to the band playing Mexican music from the gazebo. I didn't dance, though. I had no one to dance with. Maybe I was too afraid. It was beautiful, the dancing in the town center, the lights of the city behind them, the music, the men in cowboy hats and their women.

When I went into the hotel restaurant that first night to order some food at the bar, the bartender came over to me and asked, "*Quieres una cerveza?*"

He threw me off guard. The wandering I had done, the loneliness I had experienced, had made me forget the difference in language. I hadn't spoken to anyone in hours, traveling the streets of Monterrey taking in my father's hometown. I didn't feel safe all of a sudden, there in the bar with the bartender waiting for an answer.

I said, "Give me a Coke."

I didn't feel like a man asking for a Coke, at a bar, in Mexico. Men drink beer in Mexico. Not all men of course, but the ones I know do, the ones with histories like mine. He looked at me for a minute in a strange way. Then he got "*un Coke*" and came back with it and then asked if I wanted a menu.

"Yeah. I want to eat. Please. Menu."

"*Bueno.*"

He reached behind him to the counter where there sat rows of liquor bottles. He grabbed a menu and handed it to me. I took it, opened it and looked for something to eat. He walked down to the end of the bar, lit a cigarette and started talking with a cook who had come out of the kitchen to look through the dining room. They started talking and pointing me out. I sat reading the menu, trying to ignore them. They whispered something. They started to laugh.

A cockroach passed by me along the bar top and I found myself inordinately afraid of it. I tried to move it away with the edges of my menu without anyone seeing me do this. I didn't want to overreact, so I tried to be subtle. I needed to get rid of the creature. It ran around in crazy circles avoiding the menu and my attempts to ward it off. It was all legs and head. It was so big I could have sworn I saw its face, and it seemed to be laughing. It scampered away into a crack in the bar, gone into the darkness between the coolers where all the liquor was kept. I should have killed it. I don't know why I just didn't kill the thing.

"You decide?" the bartender asked.

"Yeah. I'll have the Mexican lasagna. Is it good?"

"*Muy bien*. Excellent."

"Okay. I want it to go."

He rang me up, ordered the food, and when it came, I took it up to my room to eat. I went off alone into my self-imposed silence. I ate the Mexican lasagna.

Afterward, I sat around in my room watching television and felt sick, a gnawing feeling growing in my belly. It was like my stomach was expanding. Sharp pains shot up the sides of my body. I clutched at my torso and groaned. After a while I fell asleep and had bad dreams, and then I woke up and it was dark and I felt like I was going to vomit. I lay there in my bed, at the border of being sick and not. My stomach was roiling and my mouth grew pasty. I stared at the ceiling above.

Finally, as the pain reached my threshold for tolerance, I got up, walked to the bathroom, lifted the toilet seat and crouched over the bowl. Nothing came, even after I stuck my fingers down my throat. I stood upright and looked in the mirror. I saw spittle on my chin and I looked like a madman then, my hair messy and eyes bugged out. The muscles in my neck were sharp and ferocious, the veins in my forearms huge and bulging. Seeing myself, almost like it was for the first time, I could barely discern this person, this sick person standing there. I was a foreigner.

The nurse came to my office one morning and told me that Jimmy wanted to speak with me in private. Although Jimmy was in my American Literature class, I did not necessarily know him in any personal way. He was incredibly shy, a mousy loner who hung out at the edges. He had a circle of friends; he was on the outside of the circle. They loved Jimmy very much I think, but they showed it by razzing him about his grades, his intellectual prowess and his short stature. They would shove him around, but no more seriously than older brothers who push around their little brothers. If anything, they probably would have defended the kid if a situation got hot and he was threatened.

The kid always had his hand raised to questions I asked. Early in the year, he was the only one answering questions. His passion for class and thinking helped his grade. Then he got annoying. His classmates knew he would answer any question asked, so they stopped working hard. I stopped calling on Jimmy and grew weary of him. His discomfort with people and anything outside the things he learned in his textbooks, the strangeness he had when confronting anything outside of the information we threw at them in class, made me uncomfortable.

The nurse told me, "He's having a hard time right now. He's been having anxiety attacks. He tells me he trusts you. He wants to talk to you."

This trust he had in me took me by surprise. Outside the advice I offered him on papers and tests, outside the affirmations to his additions to class discussion, I never said anything to him. He stayed away from me. I stayed away from him. He did his work. I graded it.

I told the nurse, "Okay. I don't see why not. Where is he?" I shrugged, stood up and followed her out to go see Jimmy.

He was sitting in the nurse's office on the examining table and his legs were hanging down and dangling. He smiled and waved nonchalantly.

"Hey," he said.

I was slightly irritated at his demeanor. "Jimmy, listen. What's up?"

"I've been a little nervous lately. I don't know how to explain it," he told me, chuckling a little—embarrassed, maybe.

"You want to go somewhere more private?" I asked. Silently, we walked down the hall and found an empty classroom. I followed Jimmy in and watched him sit down. It was a beautiful day outside, the sun shining through the windows, enough so that I didn't have to turn on the lights. There was a class next door that we could see through a set of doors that separated our room from the other. The teacher was lecturing about something I couldn't quite make out. A few students saw us in the room and tried to get a better view. They thought Jimmy was in trouble.

I turned away and Jimmy and I silently stared at one another. To break the silence, I sat down and said, "Jimmy, you have to relax. I know you study a lot and care very much about your studies, but you need to figure out a way to let go. Do you know what I mean? Your work ethic, while admirable, will ultimately catch up with you."

"I don't think it has anything to do with my studying," he said. He looked at me until I couldn't hold the stare any longer and looked away. He said, "I think I might be afraid of dying. I don't know what it is exactly, or even what I mean by it, but I always dream about it. Sometimes when I'm studying I'll have these visions of my entire family being wiped away. When I come to, I yell for my mom. When she answers, I feel better."

He stopped and stared at the floor. He looked back at me. "Weird. Right?"

He smiled at me. The thick eyebrows that ran almost continuously from one temple to the other dominated his face, which was flush with acne. He hadn't shaved that day and light stubble grew high on his cheekbones.

I could tell that the wind was out of him. He started in Spanish and then stopped. Began in English and stopped. Finally, looking vaguely soothed for the moment, he said, "This one time I was at the park with my *primos* and a car pulled up alongside where we were playing basketball. We all knew what was going to happen. I looked behind us at the guys playing at the other end of the court, and wanted to yell out to them to duck, to get down. Instead, and I don't know what made me do it, I just hit the deck, man."

"You knew, Jimmy," I said. "If it was me, I would have just been shot."

"Listen," he said. "The window rolled down and I saw the guns. Here everything went slow motion and mute. I don't even remember my body going down, but it must have. I covered my ears and rolled around on the ground. I thought I could hear the bullets race through the air. I heard someone scream."

His voice trailed away. He looked out the window. He looked back at me and said, "What if I hadn't hit the ground? I'd be dead. Right?"

"Look. You can't worry about that. You didn't get hit, right?"

"I mean," he continued, interrupting me, "everyday this stuff happens, man. Look what happened to Sergio."

The name of the Garcia boy rolled off his tongue like a bomb because, while he may have looked up to his schoolmate, I didn't know that he had internalized the death. How could I? Most of my students just shrouded themselves in the apathy they know only too well, having experienced that kind of violence before.

Jimmy gestured to the west. He said, "This all happens by my house. It happens, like, every day."

"Listen to me for a minute. You aren't going to die from a gun. You just can't let yourself worry about these things."

Somewhere, deep down inside me, I knew those words meant nothing because the Garcia boy was dead. I had lied to Jimmy about being safe, and he knew I was lying.

I was looking out the window of my hotel, into the night. My father had spent his teenage years in this city. He gathered a rudimentary education, and by the time he was 16, he had run the border approximately 150 miles away. He'd been caught and deported. It was from here—endlessly wandering, moving about aimlessly, the cobblestone streets lined with row after row of tiny homes painted pink and blue, orange and yellow—that he probably planned, once again, to run. The next time, he told himself, he wouldn't be turned back. Grown up in him, in his heart, was a great fear of leaving, but he knew that if didn't he wouldn't know what living was. He understood, maybe as all of us do, the potential of being alive, but here, this place, the stink of it, stifled what he knew life could be like. My father, just a teenager, understood at the core of him some basic promise of life.

There, in Monterrey, more than 30 years later, as I looked down into the town square, I felt my dad's alienation with a place and a time. How much did he keep inside him? How many days and how many nights did he curse this place under his breath? In Monterrey, there was nothing for a young man so sure of himself and, at the same time, so unsure of his country, to fulfill the promise he felt in his gut. It was in the impossible that my father might have first sensed the possible somewhere else.

In 1971, a month before his 19th birthday, my father, the dreamer, started his way north, working odd jobs along the way to gain enough capital to get him over the border, enough capital to be able to eat and drink once an alien in the United States. He rode a bus out of some small town halfway between Monterrey and Nuevo Laredo, a dangerous machine, all exhaust and engine noise, bursting with people and hopes. He was on a collision course with my mother and a city, a place, a word, one word; a sound so foreign on his tongue, yet strange, virile, the hard opening consonants, the long easy middle vowels, the light ending floating off the tongue the way the words fall from a Spanish speaker pronouncing their I's like E's, A's like Ah's. It was a whole life he hoped for in the articulation of one word that he would never entirely pronounce right: Chicago.

I called my mother from the hotel room in Monterrey. She asked me how the trip was going.

"Good," I told her. "It's fine. I'm doing what you told me to do. I'm not expecting too much. Just looking around. Sort of passing through."

"Just passing through. Like a tourist. Good. There's no pressure in being a tourist, is there?"

"No. None," I lied to her. "No pressure. I feel like a foreigner."

"You are, Rafa," she told me, laughing. "You are a foreigner." My mother yelled out to my stepfather, Tom. "Hey, Rafa feels like a foreigner! In Mexico!" There was a rousing chorus of laughter.

"You are," she said through the giggling. "You are."

My father told me a story once when I was younger about how he had to feed the cows on the ranch when he was a boy. I had laughed because I never believed that he was from such a place, but he was. He was from a farm and had to feed pigs and cows. He told me that it was his responsibility to do it every day before the sun came up. He was afraid of the dark and had his older brothers put up a rope line that would connect the house with the barn, where the animals lived, even as they razzed him about being so afraid all the time of something as harmless as the dark.

"It was in the dark that I felt like I was losing my way," I heard my father tell me as I sat in the city he conjured up.

My father told me back then, "I always told myself to forget about the noises that I thought I heard. I told myself over and over again to ignore it, what I thought might be there at the edges of my vision. There is nothing there, I'd say to myself. It is only your imagination, Rafael, I'd say to myself. There is nothing to see, nothing to hear. And there I'd go, *mijo*, holding on to that rope, even when I knew exactly where I was going. I knew the way to the barn like the back of my hand, but I grew to need the rope.

"It is funny what you remember, *mijo*. I'm not sure if I really needed the rope until after my father died. I don't remember being so afraid of the ranch or the haunting or the things my own imagination could conjure up until my father was killed and he was gone from the world. To be honest, I can't remember if this happened before or after. I know this though—I felt that if I didn't have something that I could hold on to, to have guide me in all that dark, that I would just float away or be lost forever."

In the streets of Monterrey, I saw cars rumble at ungodly speeds, changing lanes, tearing through yellow caution lights at street corners. It felt like a phantom, that image of my father walking very slowly from his house to the barn, holding a rope in all that darkness, fearful of the father he never really knew. Stepping as lightly as possible because if he made too much noise he might awaken something he was not prepared to deal with yet. More than that, the image I had of my father as a boy was not of him walking along lightly with his hand on the rope, but hanging on for dear life, as if he were climbing up the side of a very steep cliff, his muscles taut as he used both hands to maneuver in all that dark, going from one place to another, praying that the ugly thing his mind was conjuring up would go away forever.

One day as he was sitting in my office after school, Jimmy asked me out of the blue, "Do you ever think that your education is bad? I mean that somehow, by taking in all that you want me to take in, and through my memorization of it, I am losing my place in my own family. I have lived in a quiet house all my life—well, ever since my family stopped speaking Spanish so my brothers and sisters and I could get ahead. Without even me asking, I lost a little bit of my family. It seems like what I'm learning is making me crazier and lonelier than I was before."

"You're not crazy, Jimmy. You're thinking hard about what your education is about. You're thinking hard about the things we have taught you and the effect it has had on your family."

I was recording all the detentions I had received from teachers that day. I looked at Jimmy, and he was slouched over in his chair trying to balance a pencil on the tip of his middle finger. His eyes were crossed from the focus. The pencil kept falling to the floor, and he would bend down to pick it up, only to have it fall again.

I said, "Yes, I suppose you're right. You're losing a lot. All of the time."

"It hurts," he said, the pencil delicately balancing there on the tip of his finger for a second. "I'm moving away from my parents. I can't be stopped. It's a done deal." With that the pencil fell to the floor and he let it lie. He looked at me defiantly.

I said nothing. I couldn't argue with him.

It wasn't a total disappointment, the trip down there. Wandering around among the people, feeling out my own foreignness, I realized that I didn't have to be haunted anymore about my father or the thing he came from, which I came from, too. Having crossed the border, I realized that my father's story and his name mean very little to me. I have made Mexico and the man my father is in my own mind. I have given it weight and meaning. I have been consumed by the memory of my father for the better part of my life, as if his spirit had glossed over everything, as if it were rubbed into the concrete and plaster of the Mexico I visited, the highways and factories on the edge of town. I am only a tourist in his world. We are equal parts stranger, he in my country and I in his.

As I rode in a taxicab racing to the airport to leave Mexico, past all the huge silos and humped modern buildings housing all the multinational corporations, so out of place in all the dust and dirt and wind, I saw a huge billboard coming fast upon me as I looked into the sky outside the window of the car. The rising sun was stunning and red behind us, casting shadows across the vast darkness that lay ahead.

In only a few hours I was back in the United States, in San Antonio. I rented a car and threw my suitcase into the trunk. I got on the highway and drove downtown, doing what I should have done from the beginning—go to Laredo, Texas, where my father crossed into the United States. I moved from lane to lane, speeding past the skyline, all the yellow, brown and black of it, all the concrete, brick and mortar of it. I raced haphazardly into the open country to the place I should have gone to before, where I was always heading because it's there that I could find my father, make sense of the man and his American life, or at least find out what went into making it whole.

The emptiness of the Hill Country sprawled out before me. Dust rose from the tracks of Union Pacific trains, a hundred cars or so, moving out into the numina of the United States. Running parallel, headed in the opposite direction, I rode south, toward the border, a line in the dirt somewhere far away. Again Mexico, a long vague locale out along the horizon, as far as the eye could see in both directions. I was being pulled there, to the heart, to the place my father crossed over. Laredo. I rolled over the desolate landscape where cattle roamed and something like epiphanies rolled sweetly over the dirt majesty of my American West like tumbleweed in the Western movies of my mind.

I went to Jimmy's graduation party. I drove over to his house in Little Village, past the empty train yards. Exhaust from the planes landing and taking off from Midway Airport streaked the sky. At 26th and California, the large looming walls of Cook County jail rose into the air, dwarfing the neighborhood. Barbed wire and lookout posts, armed guards.

Signs said, in English, "Congratulations, Jimmy!"

No one had arrived yet. The food was still cooking and Jimmy was somewhere in the house getting ready. I hung around on the back patio with his high-school-age cousins. I stood listening to them crack jokes about each other and about other guys in the neighborhood. After a while, Jimmy came from the house, nervous and awkward, loping along. He looked like his mother had dressed him and styled his hair, not with gel but with her hand after licking it. He looked sort of ridiculous and I laughed. He shot me a look. He was wearing a bright yellow shirt that was too big for his scrawny self and a huge wide-bodied black and yellow tie. He wore baggy pants that hung too low on his waist. His shoes were massive. It was like his mother dressed him up in clothes she thought he would like, not even knowing the size and tastes of her own son anymore.

We talked for a while about small things. Jimmy was nervous. His family started to trickle in and they all gave him little envelopes full of money, I'm sure. Some of them had wrapped gifts, which he took, smiled at and, after saying thank you to his aunts and uncles, set them on the ground at his feet or handed them to his brother to set on a nearby table.

I said, "Congrats, Jimmy. You ready to go?"

"No." He looked away shyly. He didn't want to have this conversation with me. He looked at the ground and began kicking at the cracks in the concrete.

I kept on. "Well, that's okay, I suppose. You'll have all summer to get ready."

"I applied to ITT, too. I might go there. They gave me a lot of financial aid." He told me about ITT for a while, and I barely listened, trying to think how the kid could possibly fathom giving up a full ride to Marquette University for an education at a small technical school where he'd learn blue-collar skills. He'd learn how to fix air conditioners, heating systems, computer applications. I thought about all the classes he'd miss out on that would fill out his life: the philosophy, the political science, the literature classes, the classes that would expand upon and illuminate the ideas he was grappling with at the end of his high school career. Was it merely fear that was motivating his decision? Was he serious?

I interrupted him. "ITT is fine, I guess, Jimmy. But it's not Marquette. You want my opinion?"

"Do I have a choice?"

"No."

"Fine. What?"

"Forget about it. Forget ITT, Jimmy. It's not a real education. Sure, it's okay for some, but you've been given something great, a scholarship to study at one of the best Jesuit universities in the United States. You'd be a fool to skip out on that."

"I won't fit in," Jimmy said.

"You will fit in. White. Black, yellow. No one fits in, man. No one likes leaving mom and dad. You fit in," I said. "You're an American."

He laughed a little, ironically. "Yeah. I guess," he said. "Okay."

"You better go."

"I don't know."

"You go."

"Maybe."

The northern edge of Laredo looked like the abnormal spawn of Los Angeles' South Bay. It was full of strip malls and palm trees. Everything was covered in exhaust and to get from one end of the city to the other required a biblical patience. The amount of sun and the heat that came with it felt like it was invading my privacy. Billboards stood all alongside the highways and Spanish radio blared from car stereos. Oil wells dotted the horizon along with cheap motels. The freeway was flooded with cars headed south to Mexico. Traffic jams northbound, people headed out, coming back from the other side. The desert licked at the city limits.

Sitting in traffic, a grueling four-lane freeze, and looking at a map, I stared at the vast empty spaces where Mexico and the United States were divided by a thick, 4-millimeter line that represented the river my father swam more than 30 years ago. Out against the river, on the American side of the map, streets twisted like those in the subdivision of a suburb. Down along the border, near the traditional points of entry, bridges one and two, the streets flopped onto one another, crammed together. Highway 35 ended in the downtown of a stifled border town. Like a zombie, I parked my rental car in a parking lot in Laredo, Texas. Across the river there was Mexico, yellow lit and ferocious, a cacophony of noise. I walked to her, crossed the checkpoint on the bridge. Halfway across, I stopped and tried to imagine what my father saw that one night in those moments that are such a part of our familial myth that it seemed like it didn't even happen. Like the undead, alone, I walked on.

He found himself in M. Carpenter Hall, the kid who's afraid of dying. The kid who's afraid of change found himself at the corner of 11th Street and West Wisconsin Avenue in Milwaukee. His dorm room overlooked the sprawling exit ramps of highways 43 and 94 out of Chicago, north to places he didn't even know about, places as far away as he felt, only an hour and a half from Little Village.

The way I picture it, he spent a lot of time walking about and taking in the sights of his new city, all the white faces with pink mouths speaking crisp, clear English. He wandered around the quads between 16th and 11th, massive spaces that made him feel tiny and insignificant, with their tall white buildings, trees everywhere, indescribable for the child of Mexican immigrants. He walked long distances, past parking structures on Wells Street, past libraries and under the overpasses of the major freeways, the high abstract noise of speeding cars above his head. Most days he felt overwhelmed, a young man amid the known, but aching in the heart by an alienation that was tied to being there among the unknown, the impersonal. Having walked in the American city, this son of immigrants, having spent his early years masking an essentialness, he no longer knew who he was.

He walked farther downtown, past the Bradley Center, past steel bridges that straddled the Milwaukee River. The kid walked and walked. There was industry in the south and tourist traps in the north. Some days he sat in the park along Lake Michigan and watched the boats out at the middle of the lake, far away it seemed, a mirage almost on the top of a lake that sparkled like a million little diamonds having been thrown into the air and scattered. An American city behind him, a place where there may be answers but always, still more questions rising, like the skyscrapers and cranes above, stone on stone, always more land to unearth and build on. America, his country, cool angles, mean streets.

Sitting there, in the hard shine of the sun, before the classes Jimmy Barajas felt completely unprepared for, he thought hard about what it took to get there and what it would be like to leave it behind, go home and deal with what he considered to be safe. He thought hard about being there, not only in Milwaukee, but also being there in the world. There was still time to drop out, he thought to himself. I could leave this place. I could go home. Sitting there, desperate and scared, the realization came upon him that he may not even know where home was anymore.

The No. 1 song on the charts in April 1972 was "A Horse With No Name" by the band America. It came barreling out of the bars lining Avenida Guerrero. Rock music surrounded my father, Rafael Garcia, as he moved through the broken streets, at the edge of the border town. In the distance he sees the lights of Texas. They are calling him, challenging him.

The way I picture it, the streets were strewn with Coca-Cola bottles, crushed cigarettes. A wretched smell rose into the air, the mixture of garbage and sweat. Trash toppled out from the houses out in the avenues and boulevards, wrapped itself around telephone poles, washed up against crowded bus stops, around the people who slept in the streets, out into the underbrush at the edges of the town, against the massive fence that ran in either direction down near the river. Buses moved the congestion of bodies and smells back and forth over the city, crowds of wranglers and working-class people, toughs in cowboy hats who had worked on the other side, hustlers in leather pants with crimson faces and limp wrists, the pregnant and anonymous moon-faced women with children at their legs under the stifled heat of the border town, moving them back and forth over the insufferable little streets, house upon house, place upon place.

My father moved about quick-footed, waiting for dark. An invisible man amid all the invisibles and anonymous and nameless. His story was all stories. He was going to America to be somebody. Little did he know, this young, drifter kid.

There was a small courtyard about three blocks from the international border. In the center, people milled about, waiting. The whole place a middle ground. What is the word for the process or condition of purification in which those who die are made ready for heaven?

With them, my dad, 19 years old, rambled about, standing around, sitting down. He spent some of his money on beer, toasting away his past, all that land to the south, wild and dangerous, the thing he'd try to keep secret until his oldest son would ask him about it years later after holding it in for so long.

He sat in lonely, forlorn bars out on the edge of it all, past the bright lights of the tourist traps, the strip clubs, the gambling halls, past the piñatas for sale, the Virgin of Guadalupe towels, the general kitsch of the border town. He was down in it, alone and restless. He was going to leave his own country. He thought he would return one day, but he would not. He was part of the American mind and he hadn't even crossed over yet, run the border, jumped the wire. My old man hadn't even gotten wet behind the ears. American kitsch. Drinking, in my mind, at 19 years old, my father was like something I would win at a carnival.

He'd arrived two days earlier and spent his time sitting in a cheap hotel along Guerrero. Hotel Texas it was called, a low-down dirty dive of a place with a lightbulb hanging from the ceiling, dangling there, swinging if the people upstairs moved around too much. The whole place felt like it was going to cave in from the weight of the people, the inertia of all that waiting going on. In the corner of the room, there was a sink for when he was dirty, and for when he was tired, a mattress on a cheap metal frame along a wall near the window. He was to supply his own sheets and didn't have them, so he slept in his clothes and his boots. The window that overlooked a well-populated little piazza didn't close all the way. From the square there were all-night howls and cries, car horns from the street. Who cares? He was excited, jacked on an idea, a faraway place, a place he had heard about only in books and from relatives and friends. Who cares, car horns and yowling? Who cares, hookers and pimps and hustlers? Who cares?

He spent time walking out along the road near the fence, near the river, eyeing it, trying to memorize it, the contours of the thing. It moved quickly around in a bend downriver. He sensed that it was deep where he would cross, under the bridge for pedestrians. Others had begun to congregate at the edge. Across the river, about a quarter of a mile away, the greasy lights of Texas shone in the dark sky like jewels that someone had thrown up over their head and let fall in a fit of panic or religious exuberance. The water glimmered. Rafael, my father, waited. He eyed the lonely patrol across the river, took care to remember how they moved, when they moved, and what they were like.

As I imagine it, he moved out into the bushes on the other side of the road, the last road in Mexico. Above the runners the bridge swarmed with tourists. There were American men in cowboy hats and cheap T-shirts with sunburned arms. The American girls' asses wagged in tight khaki shorts and their expensive purses hung from freckled shoulders, some of them sunburned. They stood and watched, rambled around. The runners hated them because all they wanted was a little peace and quiet. They were going to leave their country, a little solitude would be all right.

They moved in closer to the swampy area at river's edge. Right there in the middle, my father, a person most Americans deny, was everything they find difficult to come to terms with.

The runners are the people all Americans keep secret, for they are the memory of their own familial lives and past tribulations, the coming-to-America, a drama being played out in every border town every night of the week all year round. Listen. It is happening right now, just like it happened to my father, the Mexican, the wetback. He was young out there in the swamp, in the stink, brown-faced and eager. In a few hours he would be running through the heartland of America because something deep inside of him, something he couldn't articulate, told him he should leave his country, forge ahead, make something new out of the old, a young man who grew up without a father, the memory of a father, a father who beat him and tortured him more in his absence than when he was alive. He had a murderer for a brother and a mother who could do nothing for him but pray and pray and pray.

Up where the tourists dwelled, old Mexican women sold hard candy with jalapeños in the middle. They sold Mexican Day of the Dead skeletons, leather belts with brass buckles that said "Mexico." Everyone and everything was ironic there. Everything was like an eternal joke each country had for the other. Both sides played their roles in overdrive. The border was America on steroids, was Mexico drunk on tequila.

In the dark he heard, "You see, I've been through the desert on a horse with no name. In the desert, you can remember your name."

My father pressed his boots into the mud. The water rose and swallowed his foot. Ahead of him, across the river in a city hundreds of miles away, waited a woman he didn't know yet, slinging drinks by night in a bar on Rush Street, working by day as a secretary in an advertising firm on South Wacker Drive, where the Sears Tower was rising slowly but surely, level by level, monstrous cranes pulling up iron and steel to dizzying new heights.

6

FEARLESS MORAL INVENTORY

2000/2004

The fourth step of Alcoholics Anonymous reads, "Make a searching and fearless moral inventory of ourselves." Alcoholics new to the program, those who stay, must complete this step to move on to the last eight. This step asks us to find all that is wrong with us, all the things we ever did that were wrong, morally wicked and psychologically twisted and to write them all down for the world to see. The program asks for a list. It is in this act that we can "clean our side of the street," my sponsor says to me. I have one month's worth of sobriety.

It's early 2000 and I've come home again to Cleveland and it's snowing lightly. There are big, heavy flurries. It's gray out. It's Cleveland. It's just after the New Year.

I'm reading that line, the fourth step, over and over again in a small diner near my mother's house. The fluorescent lights are stained yellow; smoke rises from the griddle across the counter and seeps up into the air, staining the ceiling and giving me a headache. I smell the bacon fat. From where I'm sitting I watch someone shovel food into their mouth, eggs and hash browns, and it makes me want to vomit.

I ask Mike, "What do you mean keep my side of the street clean? What does that mean, make a searching and fearless moral inventory? Do you want me to write this down, show you? This list?"

"Yeah. You'll show me and read it to me, all the little things you did. You got to be totally, brutally honest with yourself. Show yourself. Be naked, kind of."

Mike's a smoker. He's on his fifth cigarette in the last hour. He's drunk the same number of cups of coffee in half the time. He's high-strung, a recovering addict through and through. He tells me his story every time I see him. He's sober because he got caught writing prescriptions for other addicts. It earned him seven felonies. He got sober because he couldn't do it anymore: smoke crack, drink, write false prescriptions, go to jail, almost die over and over again. He's got five years of sobriety. I've got 30 days. One fucking month and I want a drink, not this searching and fearless moral inventory of myself bullshit.

Searching and Fearless Moral Inventory of Myself: all the girls, the hopeless relationships, the demise of any semblance of family happiness. All the money I've stolen from friends, families and lovers. The cars wrecked, five, maybe six. I forget. The peace disturbed. The week in Greene County Jail in Xenia, Ohio (what would have been 63 days had my stepfather, Tom, not intervened, convinced my mom I had had enough). The two felonies, the warrants for arrest, that hang over my head—drug possession, heroin and coke—this is impossible.

Mike tells me, bringing me out of my dream, always the same dream: old dark bar with the lonely, disconnected drinking. After, I get in my car and drive home and half in blackout and maybe half not…there's a telephone pole…then a broken nose. It's the kind of dream where you're sledding down a hill at top speed and you know it's too much and you make no move to stop it. The velocity, there's something hyper about it, the excitement, the nerve, the moxie of it, you don't stop though in your dream, in real life—all of it so much the same—you never stop and then as you're going to fly off the cliff, fly off the edge of the world, the very precipice separating you from the blank, the void, the nothing, you wake up.

Mike whispers, "You have to get your side of the street clean. You got to hand it over to a power higher than yourself, God, Buddha, AA, whatever, man. You got to get yourself clean. You've got to get honest with yourself, brother."

He smokes. I smoke.

I move to talk. He says, "Don't say anything. Shut up."

I make a face like I hate him, which I do. But he's the closest thing I've got to a friend. I hate him. Fearless and Moral Inventory.

Mike says, sipping a bit of his coffee, "Listen, man. Turn to page 64."

He wants me to read from a book I have some experience with. I know its insides from other times on the wagon. When I was 19 I had been through this kind of thing after I wrecked my first car. I was driving north in a southbound lane on some random Cleveland street. At the time I was a college dropout, drinking from Thursdays to Sundays, working 7 in the morning to 3 at a McDonald's five days a week. I was definitely a sad case and headed nowhere fast, already dabbling in cocaine, which would tear me down later on.

What I remember the most about that night was the lights from the police cars. There must have been seven or eight cop cars. I came out of the blackout and into the ferocious blast of white light from the headlights of their cars, which surrounded my own, which was up on the tree lawn of someone's property crammed up against a tree. I was about 100 feet from their bay windows, their living room, 100 feet from possibly smashing through the glass and brick of their home. As I stepped out into the light a police officer asked me gruffly, "Son, do you know where you are?"

I looked around and told him the street intersections I thought I was at.

He told me, "Close enough." He yelled out to the other guys, "He's loaded. No need to test him. We'll give him the Breathalyzer down at the station."

On the way to the station when I told the officer, in hopes he'd let me out, "I need to quit drinking. I think I'm an alcoholic, sir."

He told me, "Well, son, that's the first step. You should go to a meeting."

Looking back, I think that was the first time I had ever told anyone I was an alcoholic. This cop, the first cop who'd ever arrested me.

As part of my first DUI conviction and probation, in lieu of jail, I was to spend many months in an outpatient program at a drug rehab center. It was there, in those groups and meetings I was forced to go to every night, that I got my first real taste of the Big Book, its stories of suffering and recovery, its triumphs and defeats. In that volume, I came across the important life-affirming 150 pages that made up the first edition of the book, written so long ago, in 1939 by two drunks named Bill and Bob, a failed businessman and a doctor who helped each other get sober, stay sober, and then arm themselves with a spirituality by spreading the good word to others still sick, others still suffering, calling them out, ending the madness of others' alcoholism. I stayed sober that whole time, six months total. The next week, after I was done with rehab, I went out with a guy from the group and started drinking again. I would spend the next six years moving fast in a downward spiral of booze and drugs. Yet, because of that book ingrained in my head I never quite drank the same, the truth of the Big Book rolling around in my head every time I picked up a drink.

"Read. Second full paragraph," Mike says to me, pointing into my book, clutching his coffee mug.

I read silently to myself.

"Out loud, smartass."

I read, "We did exactly the same thing with our lives. We took stock honestly. First we searched out the flaws in our make-up which caused our failure. Being convinced that self, manifested in various ways, was what had defeated us, we considered its common manifestations."

There's banter in the diner, the sound of silverware and plates, coffee cups and saucers. A cockroach crawls from the window to the dark below, beneath our table.

I look at Mike's book, the yellow worn-out pages, the high-lighted marks, the pen and pencil in the margins. He's studied this thing, this book. I look at my book, at its clean, brand new pages, the spine barely broken. I want my book to be like his book. I don't have a pen or anything.

Mike says, "Resentment is the No. 1 offender. It destroys us, man. It's a spiritual disease we got. I got. You got." He points at me. His cigarette is a few inches from my face. Mike's leaning close. He's mean. I want a drink. Thunderbird. A 22 of Rolling Rock. A glass of vodka. Nothing special. Something swift. Something senseless. I want a big fat rock. Twenty dollars' worth. A nice megasized pipe full, crusted with the yellow residue of past use and a piece of Brillo near the tip, wedged into it, behind the rock, to take away the impurities as I inhale. I want to get to the essence of that rock, the smoke, the sweet smoke, the sweet-ness on my lips. The heavy smoke. The purity of the smoke. The rush. The high. The allure. The way my body loses itself. The way my dick gets hard. The way it goes soft again, forever and ever, always impotent, emotionally, physically. Empty. Empty. Empty. The way my eyes flutter, head falls back. The way. The way. The way I just want to feel okay, 10 minutes' worth, then the comedown. More.

Searching and Fearless Moral Inventory. One month sober.

Alejandro sits in the back seat of the police cruiser with a shirt and tie on, baldheaded and handcuffed. *60 Minutes* is filming away. You can hear the whir and hum of the camera. The man behind it is shooting the back of Alejandro's head. There's a sound man behind the cameraman, his microphone in the air, aimed down at me.

The crew of this CBS show is here to do a piece about a high-achieving inner-city high school, and they've been interviewing me about the students here, about the death of the Garcia boy, the gang stories, the way we shape students, how I try to steer them clear of the streets, the allure, the addiction of it all. But right now I'm yelling to the other students, the students filing out of the graduation ceremony, Class of 2004. I'm yelling, "Go home. Get out of here. There's nothing to see," I yell, looking at what they're looking at, what *60 Minutes* is looking at, what others are looking at. I yell, "Get out of here."

I threaten detentions for the younger students. I'm ridiculous out here in the frame. Ridiculous out here in the heat, in the suit I'm wearing. Moments away from a riot, I rely on the detentions in my pocket to keep security, as protection against chaos. They stare at me then into the police cruiser.

The arresting officer is taking names, notes, asking questions. He has a billy club out, his gun holstered. His partner's got his own hand resting on the butt of the 9 millimeter he carries on his waist. They're wearing bulletproof vests. It's quite a scene. A fantastic mix of joy and fever, joy for the graduates, fever because of the spic in the back of the cop car, lights of four or five cop cars whirling in broad daylight.

There are at least 300 people now in the courtyard. The sun is burning. People are wearing sunglasses, women in flower print dresses. Men in suits clutch at their necks, some loosen ties, others grin and bear it. People fan themselves. Cameras everywhere. There are balloons in the air; people are taking pictures, the happy graduates and their families. The full courtyard. The Latin King in the back seat of the police cruiser.

Alejandro is arrested for trespassing because I called the cops on him. Two months earlier I had kicked him out of school; two months before he was to earn a diploma from the school with his girlfriend, who he has come to see today, to get one little picture with her, a hug, a smile.

The reporter for *60 Minutes* asks me, the camera in my face, the microphone above my head, the students clustering near, "Do you think this was necessary? What does this prove?"

The camera is rolling. Alejandro is framed, I think, perfectly behind me. The money shot: me, the dean of students who kicked out Alejandro in the foreground, the gangbanger, the Latin King, in the background, looking out through the windows of the cruiser.

I tell her, "I don't want to talk now. Now's not a good time."

She says, "What does this prove? Wasn't this a little overdone? The Chicago Police Department? He just wanted to see his girlfriend, right?"

I think she is right. I feel sick with hypocrisy on these kinds of days when my job efficacy is questioned. Let's face it, this is the most ironic thing I could possibly be doing ever in my life. It's like I'm repaying some cosmic debt by entering into the lives of troubled youth. I want to tell her, "Yeah, it sucks, I had to get him arrested but he knew he wasn't allowed back. I had kicked him out for gang involvement." I want to tell her, "There's a history here. Other things have happened with him. I have saved his ass numerous other times, defending him when he should have been kicked out before, when others called for it. It isn't as simple as it looks." I want to tell her, "If I let him in there, with the others, his friends and his girlfriend, what does that say about our zero tolerance policy?" I want to tell her that my past, and her knowledge of it, doesn't make a goddamned bit of difference because this is my job. I have to keep other people safe. The school has to do this, and I am its spokesman in the discipline department. I want to tell her that every time there are known gangbangers in the area there's the possibility for serious life-altering danger.

A week earlier I did a full interview with the whole *60 Minutes* news team. I talked about how the school sent a clear message to the neighborhood regarding gangs. I told them about the need to have these kids learn a sense of personal responsibility.

I said things like, "My boys here need to understand that the world is hard and that they have choices and that they need to always make the right choices. I'm hard on them because I care about them." I said, to the award-winning journalist, me with makeup on, "Learning now, these hard things about life, what's right and wrong, makes it easier later on. I know what living hard is like. I wish I had had someone kick me around a little bit."

She asked, the big journalist, she asked the tough question, "So, you're a recovering alcoholic, you've been in jail—"

There was a second or two of silence. A cameraman looked at me from behind his camera, then peeked into the viewfinder, saw me through his little screen and then looked back at me in real life. I thought I noticed him smiling at me out there in the dark, behind the umbrella lights drooping over our heads.

"A couple of DUIs. I have been in jail, yes. County. I learned my lesson. I don't want these boys to go through that, the pain. The needless stuff of growing up."

I lied. I didn't tell her about the time they found the heroin and the cocaine in my dorm room, the subsequent arrest, the $10,000 bond my mom put up so I could continue to study at Antioch College, instead of simply doing time in lockup.

On the morning I threw him out of school, Alejandro was like a movie rushing into my office. He's a little guy, maybe 5 foot 2, a strong 130 pounds. He's good-looking. In his shirt-and-tie dress code he's figured out ways to represent his gang colors, gold and black.

I was sitting at my desk. The first bell had rung 20 minutes earlier. Since he was late, he needed to come to my office for a pass. Instead, he told me he needed to park his car in the employee lot, in the garage under the gym.

I asked him, "Why? Why do you need to?"

No student had ever asked to do this, so I was sort of in the no man's land of rules. Was it against the regulations to let a student park in the lot? I mean, it wasn't as if there was no room. Alejandro was a good kid, I thought, besides the few times he'd had a run-in with the rival gangs in the neighborhood. "The bigger question is," I told him, "why are you late? It's 8:25, man. What's up? Where you been?"

"Yeah. Sorry." His eyes were bloodshot. It looked like he'd been crying. His face was red. His hands were buried in the pocket of his jacket. I leaned back in my chair and looked him up and down.

"What did you do?" I said. "Why do you need to hide the car?"

"Nothing happened, really. I just got chased to the school

by another gangbanger. An SD. I don't want them to see the car, to screw it up even more."

He was talking about the Satan Disciples, one of the rivals of the Latin Kings. For a year now I had heard rumors about Alejandro's gang involvement. There was the time at the end of his junior year when he was at the corner of Cermak and Western and his girlfriend had run into a taqueria to get them some food. When she came out, two SDs were pulling him out of the car, through the window. They beat him senseless. The next day he had scrapes and bruises on his body, his arms, his legs. He had a huge black eye. I questioned him that day. He told me that it wasn't that big of a deal. It was a case of mistaken identity, he said.

"You aren't a gangbanger then?"

"Naw. Not me. I know some, but not me. They thought I was someone I wasn't."

I'd left it at that and made a mental note to watch him, keep an eye on him, not to make his life miserable but to make sure to talk to him more. I knew then that he was a banger. He was always shaving his head, the No. 1 way to get on the wrong foot with me as dean. Baldhead equals Gang Activity, like it or not. So do bruises and shiners and colors, gold/black, blue/black, red/black.

Six hours after Alejandro asked to park in the employee's lot, I kicked him out of school.

It's been seven months since then, and now he's sitting in my apartment. We got back in touch because a colleague of mine, Alejandro's old homeroom teacher, got an email asking for my email address. My colleague asked me, and I told him sure, give it to him. I was curious about what he wanted and had thought a lot about what happened. I still cared for the kid.

His first email began, "WAZ UP, MR. TORCH? BEEN A LONG TIME…" Why did he want to see me? I didn't know. I think he thought I was his friend. But even so, I was afraid of him coming here. What if it was a hoax? What if he came with guns blazing, getting revenge? I kept thinking I was so stupid giving him my home address, allowing him into my home, but I think he saw me as someone who could help him.

He tells me, both of us sitting there, me on the couch, he across the room in my recliner, watching the Yankees-Twins play-off game, "I don't want you to think I'm a thug. I'm good."

I tell him, "No, I don't think you're a thug. I know you're good. I just don't understand why you've got to do this to yourself. Why do you do it? What is so alluring?"

"Do you like me? I'm afraid you might not like me," he says. "I'm afraid that you think bad of me."

I tell him that when my mother used to yell and freak out at me after something ridiculous and dumb I used to do, she would say, "I hate that you're an alcoholic. I hate your choices. I don't hate *you*."

We both sit in silence for a while after that and watch the pitcher toss fastballs over the plate, over the corners, hard breaking balls that snap into the leather of the catcher's mitt. Alejandro takes a swig of the Coca-Cola I gave him. I light a cigarette and blow smoke out the open window that overlooks 18th Street.

He breaks the silence: "Do you want to hear how I joined the Latin Kings?"

And I think, A Searching and Fearless Moral Inventory.

On the seventh day of a riotous bender I forget most of, I got into my car and drove to the bar in town. In Yellow Springs, Ohio, there aren't many places to go to drink; only two bars and

I always went to the one around the corner. There were some students there that night. I remember hitting on a few girls from campus and them laughing at all my corny jokes because I could be a real charming drunk. We drank tequila and then I had a gin and tonic and then I had a beer, forget which kind, and then I had another shot of tequila and then a Long Island iced tea and then, to chase that, another beer and this kind of thing kept happening and I would find myself talking and then sleeping and then drinking and then laughing and then nothing and then I'm driving the car with a buddy of mine I met up with at the place, who was just as loaded as me.

I came to and my nose was bloody and I thought I busted it and it's the second day of the 12th month in the 2000th year of our Lord Jesus Christ and if this pole didn't stop me I would've been a million little pieces of charred flesh because straight ahead, not more than 30 feet away, were three gas pumps at the Speedway gas station.

Connor, my two-fisted drinking son of a bitch Irish friend, told me, nice and cool, "Hey listen, man." He said, "Hey listen, man. I bit a part of my tongue off."

I told him, "Well, I think I broke my nose, so fuck you. Help me get this car off the pole. C'mon, before the cops come."

He said, "No, seriously. Look." He opened his mouth and stuck out his tongue. There was a place where a tongue should have been, but instead there was only blood and so I didn't really know if there was anything missing because it was all blood and it was on the upholstery and on his coat and in his hands. My nose hurt a lot and I thought his mouth dilemma wasn't all that important, because I needed to get out of there. I had thought about running away, far far far away, and then I thought the cops would have simply looked up the license plate number and then I'd have been caught anyway. So I thought I might as well try to push the fucking two-odd tons of steel off the pole, which its front fender was wrapped around.

I had put the car in reverse and stepped into the clutch and eased into the accelerator. Nothing worked. The tires spun until I saw steam coming from the back, through my side mirror. The smell of burning rubber was strong and irritating. I threw the stick into neutral, opened the door, and fell out of the car.

It was cold and the air was like glass. I took a deep breath and coughed. It was so quiet out, like nothing. The din from the edges of town came circling in on us. There were no cars coming down the street. It was eerie. I stood there for a moment and looked at everything totally sober, like the drunk had been knocked out of me. I stood there and looked around and there were ice crystals in the trees and when the streetlights shined on them and made a web of crystal like jewels I thought it was the most beautiful thing I had ever seen. It was so fragile and heart-stopping and wonderful and I stared into it for a few moments and everything stopped around me. I thought I was dangerous for a minute but then I came to, and the noise of the street came back, the sound of cars out in the distance.

I said, out loud, trying to push the vehicle off a pole, it steaming and puttering, I said, "Listen, man. We got to get out of here. We got to go home. At all costs."

Connor said, getting out of the car, one drunk leg at a time, "I bit my fucking tongue off. Help me look for it, will ya?"

He was looking under the seat. He was looking under the floor mat. He was searching the back seat. He was searching the creases and folds of his big winter jacket.

I told him, "Fuck your tongue, man. We got to get out of here."

Suddenly I heard, "Gentlemen, we been drinking tonight?"

I turned around. It was the big fat white cop who hated me

because him and I, well, we had met before. He was shining his flashlight into my face and I smiled big.

I said, "Oh, shit. C'mon, officer, just having a little fun. You know. Thursday night and all. Blowing off a little steam after classes and everything."

"Torch, it's Friday night. C'mere." He was with the flashlight, always with the flashlight in my face, checking my eyes. He said, "Follow my finger." He moved it back and forth from left to right and I thought I did this pretty good but beyond the light that was in my face I saw his face, all shadow and sunken.

He made me do the drunk test, the side of the road thing, where you stand with arms outstretched and lean your head back and touch your nose with your index finger, left hand to nose, right hand to nose. He made me walk a yellow parking lane line, one foot in front of the other. I stumbled through them.

I told the cop, "Hey, listen. I'm loaded. You got me. Take me away, will ya? I'm tired." In October, two months before this, they had searched my room for the drugs, the coke, the mysterious white powder. I was simply holding on to something that faintly resembled a life.

That next Monday morning, December 4, 2000, I walked into the courtroom and, after the judge called my name and asked me how I wanted to plead to the DUI charge, I told her, "Guilty."

She said, "I can't hear you."

"Guilty," I said a little louder for the whole court to hear me.

She said, "Mr. Torch. You should take a minute and think about it. I think it is in your best interest, son, considering the extreme damage you did to private property and your own car, to think hard about what you are doing. You face 90 days in county jail. Three months, Mr. Torch. You also could have a large fine, not to mention restitution to the Speedway pole you hit. So, take some time, sit over there." She pointed to a table behind me.

I was in a shirt and tie. I had shaved and combed my hair. I'd made sure not to drink the night before so I wouldn't smell like booze. I didn't think I smelled like alcohol, although I thought it was just a part of me then. I didn't really care anyway.

She handed the bailiff a sheet of paper. "Mr. Torch, if you decide to stick with your guilty plea you will need to sign this sheet. It's a waiver. With your signature, you will be saying that you have given up the right to a lawyer and the right to a fair trial. Take it and sit. I will be with you in a moment. Next on the docket," she said to the bailiff, moving along.

I took the sheet and sat. She couldn't possibly give me three months in jail, I thought. I couldn't have my mother know. I didn't want her to freak out. I just wanted to go home and try to not drink. Go home and think of a way to tell my parents I wrecked my car. The paper sat before me. The judge finished with another case. "Mr. Torch, have you made a decision?"

"Yes."

"Yes, your Honor."

"Yes, your Honor. Sorry, ma'am."

"What do you plead?"

"Guilty, your Honor."

"Okay." She sighed. "What do you do, Mr. Torch?"

"I'm a student," I told her. "At Antioch."

"Antioch College, huh?" She said it with a hint of sarcasm. The court is in Xenia, the neighboring town. It's a small, rural community, blue-collar and conservative, that sees its share of wild, long-haired, radical students coming into Xenia to get beer late at night, have marches through their town streets trying to raise awareness about the troika of oppression, Sex, Gender, Race.

"Yes, your Honor," I told her.

"Well, what do you study?"

"English. I write. I'm a writer."

"Oh, a writer. How nice."

"Your Honor?"

"Mr. Torch, I think you've made a bad decision. It's not my place to say these things that I am going to say, but I'm going to say them because I have the feeling no one has before. You will listen to me. First, I think that you've gotten away with a lot because of that charming smile of yours."

People in the audience laughed.

She continued, "I think that you've been living your life right now, due to excessive drinking, on extreme luck and your luck has run out. I think you need to get help."

"I know, your Honor. I want to get help. I plan to go to AA when I leave here. When I go home. I want to get better." I said softly, "I'm an alcoholic. I need help."

My ears rang and my face felt like it was burning.

"I know you need help. I hope this does it. I find you guilty of DUI. I sentence you to 63 days in jail. I fine you $1,000. If, by chance, you can find someone to pay it, we will let you out in five days."

She hit the hammer on the gavel, and I thought I was going to faint. A bailiff came and put cuffs on me and led me through back hallways and then outside, through the main entrance of the court building, over to central lockup across the huge central civic square where people were coming to start their day, live their lives, make their money.

Someone saw me with cuffs on and said to his friend, "That's what I call a bad day."

I've muted the television.

Alejandro says, telling me about the day he was kicked out, "I was driving to school. I had Ramon and his sister with me. I looked down, at a stop sign, to change the CD. Next thing I know a car rammed me, out of nowhere."

"How did they know, you know, that you were in a gang?"

"They just started ramming. I think they thought I was an SD. They were Ambrose."

I look at the television and there's the pitch and the batter hits it foul. The camera follows the ball. Someone in the crowd catches it and they raise their arms in celebration.

"I tried to get away," he says. "I went to Western and lost control of my car. He was still chasing me. I tried to turn the corner and that's when I hit the Expedition."

"So you were driving, trying to get away and you hit a car yourself?"

"Yeah. The Expedition just took off. He went one way. I went the other. I drove through the AutoZone at Western. I'm still being chased, right. I sped along down Cermak, to Damen. I turned and then I was near the police station at 22nd Place and Damen, near the school. The guy quit me then. I parked the car outside the building, on Wolcott. You know, you came out to check the damage. Right front fender busted, rims bent.

"I wasn't even thinking when I came in to talk to you," he says.

After that, after he came to my office and we both went out into the street to look at the car, I remember I told him he should go to class. I told him that what I really thought he should do was to drive the car home, risk another high-speed chase and then come back, on the bus, risking a run-in with the SD or whatever gang that is against the Kings. But I didn't make him do that. I couldn't.

I sat for a long time thinking about what I should do. He came looking for help. He came to me before anyone else looking for help. He risked the possible consequences to ask for assistance. He was a smart kid, just like the Garcia boy. He knew what I could do, what I may do. I hated him then, at that moment. I hated him for putting me in a position of having to make a decision about his future here. He was driving two of our other students with him. They were innocent bystanders. They were nothing, just two kids who got a ride in the mornings from Alejandro. They were quiet kids. Doing nothing. No colors. No gangs. No symbols. No guns or drugs or high-speed car chases for them. But Alejandro put them in that position. When Alejandro pulled up in front of the school with his marked car, he put the whole school in the middle of some false turf war. The whole school wore the colors, had the guns, the high-speed car chases. I had given him chances before. Should I have given him another chance? God, how I remember that hour before I walked into the principal's office to tell her what had happened. I could have kept it quiet, but what would that have done for him? How would that have helped him?

I was in lockup. The sheriff told us that the computers were broken. "No one's getting booked," he said.

I was sitting in a room, a little space maybe 20 feet by 30 feet. I kept telling the sheriff I deserved a phone call. I was telling him about my rights, my due process constitutional rights. They had taken my tie, my belt, my shoelaces in case I thought about killing myself and wished to act on the impulse.

There were five guys in there and everyone was pissed. Two guys had been in there all night, and they were insane in that little room. One guy, a big pro-wrestling-type guy with a mullet, was in there for beating his wife the previous night. He said she came at him with a frying pan.

"It was self-defense, man. Self motherfucking defense."

I thought he was fried on crystal. His face was red. His eyes were large, and he was biting his fingernails until they bled, then rubbing the blood off on his pants, where there were tiny red blotches all up and down the thighs of his ragged Levis.

We stared at him and kept our distance.

I sat along the wall near the door where there was an opening in the wall, mailbox big, that they used to send us our lunches, a pile of meat, a pile of starch and a pile of sugar and syrup like peaches. And milk. My stomach grumbled and roiled.

Then the anxiety attacks set in. I had trouble breathing. I had 63 days in there, behind some huge, windowless walls and steel bars and guards watching me, and all freedom was a dream. I was still only in booking. I still had 63 full days. It was December 4, 2000, and I was not getting out until February. I would be in here for Christmas and New Year's and maybe through Valentine's Day. I couldn't breathe. The computers were broken, and I needed a drink.

Alejandro tells me he thought we wouldn't have him arrested.

"Did you know *60 Minutes* was there?"

"No."

There's silence. Then he says, "It don't matter. But. Whatever. They threw me in a cell with two D's."

"They threw you in the cell with two D's?"

"Yeah. They threw down the crown," he says. "I told them, 'Fuck you.'"

"What did they do?"

"They pushed me. We started fighting. These two guys were hitting me over and over again. I kept telling them, 'I ain't shit! I ain't shit!'"

"The cops weren't around?"

"Hell naw. They never around when you really need them."

Along the wall in the huge pod I was in at Greene County Jail, there were the telephones. I turned toward the wall because I was almost crying. I listened to the ring tone. I kept thinking, you can't cry in jail. You can't cry in jail, man. I stifled the sobs coming up in my throat. I banged my head against the wall just to make myself feel something other than that. It was then that I realized this was what I had done for the last ten years of my life, so I stopped banging my head on the wall, coolly and calmly, and just fucking let myself cry because I didn't fucking care anymore. Let them kick me around, beat me, annihilate, humiliate me. I don't care, God.

I waited for my mother to answer the phone. I waited for the recorded message to come on and tell her that she is receiving a collect call from a prisoner at Greene County Jail and, "Will you accept the charges?"

The first time I had called my mother, she hung up on me. She said into the phone, into the recorded message, "No. I will not. No."

The message said, in a cheerful recorded monotone, "Caller, the charges have not been accepted. Please hang up and try again later." I had to turn around back into the room I shared with 44 other men totally alone and disconnected from the outside word.

In the pod there were 45 cots and showers all along the eastern side, wide open to the whole room. The cots were along the north and west walls. Along the southern wall there was a guard desk and behind it the deputy sheriff. Behind him was the door. In the middle of the room there were at least 20 stainless steel tables bolted to the floor, and four chairs to each table, also bolted to the ground. This was where we went when the lights came on for morning count and breakfast. After count we had to clean our bunks, make our beds and then undergo searches by the sheriffs who tore everything apart again. We ate our meals and sometimes chilled here during the day. We couldn't leave the table until we were told to go. I sat with three old men, white hair guys, lifetime drunks. Guys who weren't ever getting sober.

Some of the guys walked around the room endlessly, some alone, some chatting with others. There were windows in there, so at least we could see the sky and the trees and some hills. There was a WalMart down the way, the big blue sign. It said "WalMart." There was barbed wire, of course, out along the top of a big fence.

Now, waiting for my mother to answer the phone, I kept my eyes to the ground. I hadn't looked anybody in the eyes in days.

This time, she answered. The recorded message came on and said its thing. This time, my mother said, "Yes. I will."

"Mom?" I said, maybe too loudly. I turned around to see if anyone heard me. The recorded message said, "Thank you. Caller, you are free to talk."

"Mom? Mom?" The phone clicked and there was a strange silence at the other end. "Mother?"

"Hi. Hello, Rafa." She sighed. I hated it when she sighed.

She was not happy. She was totally despairing and pissed off. Her son was in jail and maybe this was exactly how she was when my father would call her from jail. "Bail me out, baby," he might have said. "Call Aurelio, get the money and get me out. Now."

It's always, for the alcoholic, about him. Always.

"Are you going to bail me out?" I said to my mother.

"I don't know," she told me. "I think I may have you stay there. Maybe you should think about it."

Then there was silence at the other end.

"I need to get out of here, Mom. It sucks. You don't even know. This is the scariest thing I have ever done."

"Good. Maybe you need to be there. This is why I may not bail you out. You should sit in there. All these years, Rafa. I am worried sick about you all the time and I think every time I hear a police siren in the middle of the night that they're coming to my house to tell me you've been killed, you're in jail, you've killed someone."

"Mom."

My mother told me, "I don't know. I don't know if I want you around anymore. Maybe it's best you stay there."

"Are you serious?"

"Very."

"Well, what the fuck am I supposed to do?"

"I don't know. See if they have meetings in there. AA. Try to stay well and out of trouble. Good luck. Rafael?"

"What?"

"I love you," she whispered before hanging up.

It was all dial tone and then it happened. I was on my knees against the wall where the fucking phones were and the guy next to me was telling his woman he loved her but I didn't think she was saying it back because he was hiding his face from me and from everyone else in this open room, this cold, open room full of men just paying their fucking dues, doing their time, finding time to do time, do nothing. I thought he was going to cry.

The cord was tangled around my arms and I was banging my head against the wall saying, "Please Father Almighty Lord my Father fucking help me you stinking motherfucker I hate you."

The 19-year-old kid holds security on weekends. Friday, Saturday and Sunday nights Alejandro's out on the street, with some of the other shorties, the younger guys. He's packing heat. Everyone takes turns. Each kid gets 30 minutes. It's mandatory. Everyone, on top of the $10 a week dues, has to hold watch. Blankly stare into the dark night, hanging out in gangways, armed to the teeth.

"That's why I liked it. Why I like it," Alejandro says.

This slip of his, his switch from past to present tense, is jarring. He looks at me and I look at him for many moments and then a horn honks out in the street, below my window, and I look at the television. He shifts his weight in the chair. His face flushes. He crosses one leg over the other, fingers the Virgen de Guadalupe medallion that hangs around his neck, over his gold Rocawear shirt, three sizes too big, hanging almost to his knees, his pants sagged and perfectly pressed.

Alejandro says, "At 12 they gave me a gun. By the time I was 13 I had all kinds of guns at my disposal. .38 specials. .357 Magnums. 9 millimeters. I've shot TEC-9's, AK-47 assault rifles."

"You do know that those are Russian assault rifles, yeah? They shoot through concrete," I ask.

"You can't miss. That's the great thing about them."

I simply stare at this kid, this ex-student of mine who now attends the University of Illinois at Chicago. He takes a photography class, a creative-writing class. He has biology and English composition.

"I have always known how to separate the gang life from my life with my girlfriend, and of course, school. I never was asked to pull a burn, though. I was always passed up for that."

"Pull a burn?"

"Kill someone."

"Well, that's good, right?"

"I had to drive a few times, though."

My mother once told me a story about my father, a story I thought about a lot when I was in jail. "We were dancing at a big club down in Little Village," she said. "We had such a good time that night. We danced and danced and it was mostly fun because I had never been down to that part of Chicago before. I was living on Rush Street then with some girlfriends and working at that bar where I met him, your father, and working by day at the advertising agency. It was all so new to me, the music and the kinds of dancing. Merengue, salsa and so on. Your father was such a good one, too. I was just this little white girl from Ohio.

The most outrageous thing we did was dance the jitterbug in high school.

"Anyway your father had had so much to drink and he could barely stand, so I told him that we needed to leave. I had to get up in the morning anyway, and I needed to be at least a little coherent. I told him that we should get a cab or have someone else drive us home. He said that that was out of the question. He was wild and singing and I was laughing and trying to sing along and he pulled my arm and we moved to the back of the car, the orange Vega I had. I told him that I was not getting into the car with him if he was going to drive. He told me that he was going to drive and that I better get in the car with him.

"And now things were starting to get ugly. He had that look—the one you get. Everything changed in the eyes. He looked sinister. He shot me this look like get in the car or else.

"I started to get in and he moved to the driver's side and that's when I got out. I ran back inside and looked for his brother Aurelio, who was with us that night.

"Aurelio drove me home and told me he would go looking for my car. A few hours later, I was woken up by the telephone. It was Rafael.

"I said, 'Where the fuck are you at?'

"And he said, 'I'm in jail and I need to get out of here. I love you. Help me.'

"The bail was around $300, and back in those days you couldn't just go to an ATM to get money out, you actually had to go inside the bank for money, to cash a check, whatever.

"I called Aurelio and told him that Rafael was in jail and he said, 'Pinche cabrón. Hijo de puta.' He said he would get some money together and then come to my house and we would go get him. It was about 3 or 4 in the morning.

"We got to the police station and paid the bail and the cop pulled me aside and asked me what I was doing with these guys.

"He said, 'The Mexican in the tank is outrageously drunk.'

"I said sorry. I said, 'He's my fiancé.'

"And the cop just stared at me. Then he said, 'Your car is totaled. Your fiancé was driving down the Eisenhower and he was going from lane to lane and we were chasing him and he just kept hitting the walls, one side to the next. The arresting officers said they never saw anything like it. Someone that drunk, driving a car. I wish you the best of luck.'

"Then he smiled politely and went to go get your father."

On the fifth day of my sentence, early in the morning, I was lying in my bunk, watching television. Breakfast had come and gone and I was sleeping off the hours, just getting by. It had been three days since I talked to my mother and she had told me good luck. The only bright spot was that yesterday I received some gifts from the outside. A few college friends had come to the jail to drop off extra socks, a journal, a book, and deposited some money into my commissary account, a whole $20. Lying there watching television I went in and out of anxiety attacks, breathing deeply, the feeling that I would be here for the full term becoming much more of an apparent reality.

I heard the guard yell, "Torch, get your shit! You're out!"

I climbed down from my bunk in total awe and gathered my things. I realized I wouldn't need any of them so I gave my bunkmate my socks and my sheets, my pillow.

In the main room I was given final papers to sign. I asked the sheriff behind the desk, "Why am I getting out?"

"All I know, kid, is that your name came up in the day's releases. Don't question it. Get your clothes."

I walked into a small closet and changed. I dropped the jail outfit into a hamper and put on my khakis and my shirt and the tie I came in with. I put on my sweater. I walked back into the main room.

I said, "Can I make a phone call?"

"No, but there's a WalMart down the road. Call there."

Outside, it was freezing. I don't know what I was expecting but it was cold and icy and snow was falling from the sky. It was eerily quiet, light traffic out in the distance. The trees were shaking lightly in the wind. The door closed behind me. I was alone and sober.

I was uneasy and strange. I lurked toward the street. I saw that we were at the very end of a cul-de-sac, out in the distance, maybe a quarter of a mile away was a shopping center. There it was, WalMart. I walked slowly at first, looking back from time to time and then eased into a light jog, and after a few minutes I was sprinting away from there, sprinting away as fast as I could, past cars coming down the street toward the jail, past new paddy wagons bringing in new prisoners, ones to fill my space, my bunk. I must have looked like a maniac, running full speed away from the low, hunched-back white building behind me, the place with the rolled-up razor wire running along its perimeter, the place with no windows, the place I learned the hard way in.

In WalMart I cashed the check I was given when I left jail, bought a phone card and called my buddy for a ride. I then called my mother and she answered and I told her I was out.

She said, "Good. Go to school. Get the quarter over. Finish your work. Then come home. There's a lot to talk about."

"Mom. Did you pay the fine?"

"Yes."

"Why?"

"We'll talk about it when you get home. Tom said I should do it. I didn't want to. I am so angry. Tom said you should be here for the holidays. He thinks you'll never do it again. I hope he's right. I pray to God."

My stepfather. Tom. The man I hated for so many years because he had many years of sobriety on him. He always told my mother that she would have to let go, let me live and if that meant let me die, then that's what it would have to be. Tom. The stepfather with years and years of this kind of experience, the guy with sobriety, the tough son of a bitch who just saved my life; the guy who married my mom when I was 13 and had to deal with her son, a drunk by 15; the guy who I wanted to fight over and over again because he was telling my mom the truth. Tom. The guy I couldn't fool, ever. I hated him. I waited for my friend to pick me up because Tom's hard-earned money set me free. His faith in me, that in jail, I would admit, somewhere in my heart of hearts, the first step of Alcoholics Anonymous, that I was powerless over alcohol and that my life had become unmanageable.

Alejandro says, "I got five brothers, man. All Kings. One's locked up doing 25 to life for murder. One's in Mexico because he can't come back because if he does the pigs'll lock his ass up. Crazy Man, my middle brother, is out in the street like Bones and Chino. Chino's a baller. He made money, mad money. He dropped out of school, but he has a 2004 Escalade, right? He's got, like, fat money. The FBI seized his house once, but they ain't got shit.

"I'm lucky. I didn't have to go through all that shit. I never had to do nothing major like smoke someone. In three years, man, I'll retire. I mean, I can get out now if I wanted to, but it's just ain't something I want to do yet. I can stop anytime I want to. I think I'd like to get out at some point though because sometimes I get so mad at these guys because they just want to get hella fucked up all the time and go get some Two Six and fuck him up. I love it and I hate it. Sometimes when I'm sitting outside, sitting with the shorties, doing security, I think this has got to be the worst thing ever. Sometimes, listening to these guys go on and on about all the crazy shit one of them has done and I know what really happened, I want to laugh in their faces. I want to laugh right in their fucking faces because I see them with these tattoos, these teardrops under their eyes, with crowns everywhere and I just think what a fucking little bitch. What a stupid fucking little bitch. Kid's like 13. You know? 13. Dumb. That's what he is. Dumb.

"I guess I wouldn't mind trying to get some kid to not join. That's what I'd like to do later in my life; to save just one fucking kid and make him not do what I done. I think that these kids out here these days don't value being a King. They don't appreciate what it is that they have. Standing outside on the corner with them I just don't think they get it. All they is is just tattoo crown and teardrop and some fucking hand sign. They like something I don't. I love it. I love it. But, boy, I really hate it, too."

I think Alejandro needs someone to tell his stuff to. He needs to make a grudge list. He's riddled with guilt. The things he's done. The shocking things. The things that are left unspoken, the things he leaves behind, the deeper and deeper he goes, the farther away from reality he moves. He's a late-stage gangbanger, I think. He's afraid I think he's a thug. And like alcoholics, that's the worst thing that could happen, having other people think you are what you actually are.

Big Mike. Mike Who Keeps Me Sober Mike calls over for the waitress, lights a smoke, and looks at me. I look out at the window to the day. The diner sits on the north side of the subway tracks at Shaker Square, a street square lined with small boutiques and bookstores, a café and a movie theater. The neighborhood around it is, to the south and west, black, and to the north and east, white and wealthy.

Lined up outside, in the cold, are people waiting for the trains that are headed downtown into Cleveland and then, on the other side of the tracks, to the east suburbs. I watch these people in their scarves and gloves and their heavy coats and I watch the snow falling down into the trench where the train slides through, the white flakes melting upon hitting the ground, the steel tracks, rusted and slick.

Mike tells me that I have to go to meetings every day for the next 90 days. I can't miss a day. If I do, he says, I'll have to find a new sponsor. Mike's no joke. Mike's the guy who'll keep me sober. Mike's a gift from God.

7

SEARCHING FOR ANSWERS

2006

Sometimes I ride through *La Villita* and blast 50 Cent. I cruise heavily and despairingly up 18th Street, cut over to Loomis. I pass alleyways and gangways, garbage cans and cheap thrill bums. The bass pounds above my ears, through my reality, and there's really nowhere to go, but I go.

The Garcia boy is an urban myth now, one of those sad stories to add to the repertoire of sad American communities at the edge of the 21st century. I see long cold cinematic shots of the dangerous remnants of buildings and broken glass and hungry murderers and hunted prey that resemble people. The Garcia boy and the music give me images of empty, half-torn-down buildings like the ones that line Roosevelt Road near Blue Island Avenue and those on North Halsted near Division, near busted, rotted-out, rusted steel bridges creaking in the ferocious summer wind sweeping up all the dust and skimming it across the top of the Chicago River. Reality sets in, and the wrecking ball waits for no one. I see empty warehouses, boarded-up homes and gutted lots where yards used to define themselves. I see desolate stretches of factories sending sulfur into the air and making the sky go black, whichever way the wind blows. At the edges of *mi barrio*, I see sterile hands meet abortive ones at blank corners, crack cocaine in balloons, the point of handshakes and greetings in a world gone idle. Over on Roosevelt, I watch a whole generation of miscarried men and women just barely functioning in and out of lanes of traffic, washing windshields with dirty rags, panhandling and looking for quick fixes from fellow dealers in stolen cars, following the parched American Dreams that have, at least on this side of town, gone dreadfully wrong. I see the profitless, almost impotent, faces of men and women lining the dull landscape of Chicago, at save-me-save-me-oh-Lord-save-me CTA stops along all the major avenues, at the feet of the rising glass homes and office buildings at the city's center where stones are thrown daily.

I sing into the faint joyous dusk of Pilsen, wild and soft pinks and purples on this western horizon, past the railyards and burned-out *tortillerias*, busted homes and bombed-out cars, I sing, hard as fuck and defiant, past cop cars and the menacing barbed wire and stone walls of Cook County Jail. I sing despite the faint, sickening smell of *chicharrons* and past the *paleta* carts ringing emptily in a strangled Chicago summer afternoon, past the *elote* men and women selling stick corn and bastard mangoes with hot sauce and chili powder. I sing. I sing as I slow up to a group of *cholos* who turn to stare at me. Their guns are drawn, and I sing to them, straight to them.

I search for answers. I search for stories, something to make sense. The Garcia boy's identity has moved past the rambunctious smile and the deep, bony laugh that irritated me more than let me in on his private jokes, his sarcasm and his fierce wit. His identity has become a hodgepodge of eschatological wisdom, stupid stories we teachers tell, and company for lonely driving sessions down the Dan Ryan through the dizzying Chicago night, pulsing and reckless in all its neon and skyscrapers. His identity becomes more than his face, it becomes that lame attempt at memory and ceremony that hangs on the walls of the school's second floor art room where he has become a mode of symbolism and gross thematic exercises involving paint and watercolor. Every time I pass it, I want to either weep or spit at it. Because all of it's fake and all of it's hopeless. And then some days, I say hello under my breath as I walk back to my office, when the sun is shining through the long, clean windows overlooking an alley facing Cermak. I say this because he, I just learned, was invited to apply for early admission at Georgetown.

His mother wants to know what this means even though he is dead and buried.

Someone, another teacher, tries to make her understand that Georgetown, an elite Jesuit school in the United States, invited him to apply for entrance into its academic world of theory and safety, its ivy-covered granite buildings rise into the sky, scratching God's kingdom with their spires—the metaphoric minds of our greatest intellects. The mother weeps and weeps, and the father asks how this could have happened. This is how these things go now. He goes on and on in broken English, "I come here from Mexico. I come here for *una buena vida* and *mijo. Mi hijo.* Who would do this?"

Many nights. Many days. Every day. Sometimes I see my father on the highway, I think, and I tell my friends, "I thought I saw my dad."

And they say, "Really, where?" And I point to where I saw him. They are interested in him. He consumes me. And we move 75 miles an hour over the Dan Ryan, the Stevenson, the Edens, the Kennedy. Sitting in traffic.

There he is. There he is not.

I dream about my father a lot these days even though we haven't spoken in years and I don't think I will ever talk to him again. I don't know if that's okay, the reality of a relationship broken not by anything either of us has done, but mostly because the time passed has gotten too big to manage, and has opened up a world of silence between us. My father is truest, most precious, in the memory I have of his stories and in the life I live in dream.

Sometimes as I drive I think about his life when he first arrived in Chicago. And every now and then, it's almost as if all that separates us fades away and I'm walking with him on those streets. You didn't even make minimum wage back then, did you, Dad? But that didn't mean the passions were dead in you, the rising you felt every time you got off the subway and headed north up Rush, lined with bars and expensive little clothing shops you couldn't ever imagine yourself or one of your kind going into. The first hard lesson of your American life was not the problem of capital. No. It rested in the way you were different and how that shaped all that you did day in and day out: paying for a subway ticket, getting something to eat, waiting for a bus, driving a car, busing a table, asking for help, sizing up women you find attractive but know are an impossibility, all that whiteness. Whiteness everywhere. You, brown. Illegal. A criminal, albeit an invisible one. And worse, you may only have been a criminal in your own head.

You never talk much, not even to that waitress at the restaurant where you both work, the one named Tari who always points to things and tries out her high school Spanish on you. You never talk because you feel it, your difference, when you speak; all the ways in which you say your vowels differently and the way your consonants are really hard and conspiratorial. Your language makes you feel dumb and dirty and rude and crude and not so heroic. It's then that you feel illegal and invisible.

Then you feel ashamed. You tell yourself you are going to lose the accent but think that's an impossibility and I know it will be. You will never lose it. If language is the last thread to the old country, you will be Mexican for the rest of your life. You can learn all the English you want, all the blessed idiosyncrasies, all the irony of the language, all the innuendos and sarcasm and still, if addressed with that Mexican accent, you are forever regulated, like it or not, to the outside, to the marginal.

You are poor as hell and sometimes can't put enough together for a decent meal, sometimes going to bed hungry and sick with empty and wonder aloud in your small shared apartment. What am I doing here? And you toss. You turn. You don't even know how to articulate the passions, so you experience it only in a kind of rising in your heart. Something elevated, an ascent. You are swept away, the neon lights and the car horns and all the pretty, slim-shouldered white women running along on high heels, their legs long and their hair like silk. They are erotic and hold more of an appeal than the ones you have known all your short life. You exotify them. You feel treacherous looking at them, desiring them. You are not any less human because of your illegal status. At any moment *La Migra* can come to wherever you are and take you away and send you back to your country forever and you would never get a chance to prove yourself in this country, this country you have heard so much about since the time you were a boy, before your father was killed. And maybe because of this, you feel a kind of energy in yourself, something exciting happening in your limbs, your mind and heart. Is this the American spirit? There's a static cling in all the lights and the signs and the strange sentences and the idiomatic digs and swipes these Americans take at one another, their middle fingers in the air, yelling, "Screw you!" It's all a magic potion, as if someone ran a wand over your eyes while you were sleeping and this is what happened when you woke up or maybe you're still dreaming, Dad. Or maybe I am and you have never woken up, hence I am just another illusion of your American Dream.

There's a dial tone and then heavy beeps as I dial his number. It's a different area code because he lives in the suburbs now. He's had enough of the rough living in city streets. Now he's settled down, with his wife and four kids, my half-brothers and sisters, in the outer ring of the Chicago suburbs. City life isn't for him anymore. He's done it, felt it. He's been overworked for the last 35 years of his life, and he's looking for trees and quiet streets and a place to raise his kids. Good schools and quality of life. Can you blame him?

"You have reached the Garcia family. We are not home right now to take your phone call but please leave us a message and we will get back to you as soon as we can."

There's a beep and then the static hum of silence. I breathe lightly into the connection and hang up.

Sam[2], the chemistry teacher, stopped me one day during lunch. "You would enjoy this," he said. I was curious. I fiddled around with a Bunsen burner. I turned on and off the gas as he began the story.

As it turns out, it was one of those stories that defined the Garcia boy for me and for Sam. He told me that the Garcia boy had come up to him one day after class and told him he knew why he had the class do all those experiments. The Garcia boy told him, "Because you want us to see all the beautiful colors they can make."

2. This is not the teacher's real name.

It's a very left-brain thing to say. Yet, we rarely, as educators, have students come up to us and tell us why they think they are learning X and Y. Some teachers might take it as an affront to them, their lesson plans and their intellects. Yet Sam was floored, ecstatic and entranced. I was numb when I heard it. It made me sink into the despair I had the days following the shooting.

The Garcia boy saw the wonder that the class was allowing him to witness, the wonder of creation. His statement allowed one teacher to see he was thinking about the method of the class. The Garcia boy, whether he knew it or not, was an active participant in his own education. He is what the Jesuits wanted, someone who will see their education as a way to get closer to witnessing that higher being, that living, freaky organism that is bigger than us.

I'm convinced he thought about all of this riding the bus, or loping self-consciously around the neighborhood, stoned and paranoid, gun battles still rhyming and rolling around in his head. "What the hell is Mr. Finnegan's chemistry class about?" he might have said to himself. The Garcia boy wasn't doing very well in that first class. He was failing, but the active thinking that was happening was superior to anyone in his class. On paper, he was average, oftentimes riding the fence between passing and failing. Intellectually, in the abstract, he was superior. A warrior. An enigma. We all thought he was a wonder boy, one of those kids who will—with a little guidance—throw off the ferocity and tumult of the street and become something. Funny, if you think about it, what does that mean—Something? Become what? Something? Something what? Other than this. What? Dead.

"Maybe a historian," one of my colleagues would have said before all of this happened and changed our lives as teachers, as parents, people working and trying to breathe what little life we have into a community that is so optimistic but seemingly on death's doorstep.

I was holding out for a literary guru of sorts. Maybe a poet. The next T.S. Eliot. Or the Mexican-American Denis Johnson. He felt the tinge of despair that was wrapped up in the lives of his friends. Every time I hear the strange refrain of our young Mexican-American lives, *pop-pop-pop*, or see preadolescent Chicano boys taking to the streets armed with vulgarity and suspicion, I get a little more cynical about it all, about the outcome of this immigrant neighborhood.

Somewhere in the distance, like always, I can make out the faint, vain pops of Glocks, somewhere over the worn-out, sun-soaked rooftops of *La Villita*. Somewhere in the distance you can hear a weeping woman, *La Llorona* of the new age, the mythical mother who sacrificed her kids and spent eternity exiled from real time by the gods, searching and searching for her children. Somewhere in the distance all the myths come true and some jacked-up baller thinks he's hard because he just smoked somebody. Past weeping women, past all the little myths of my ancient bloodlines and my new American future, always ahead of me in the way of catastrophic sunsets and world-weary billboards, I chant, slowly at first but steadily, the real chorus of my hood:

> *¡Viva México, hijos de la chingada!*[3] *¡Viva México,*
> *hijos de la chingada! ¡Viva México, hijos de la chingada!*
> *¿Que Viva?*
> *Viva México, los hijos de la chingada.*

Pure and simple, *ése*.

---

3. Here Rafael Torch is adopting a traditional Mexican battle cry, often shouted on independence day. This profane and defiant chant has complex meanings, but Torch seems to be using it to loosely translate as, "Long live the fucked-over ones." For a nuanced examination of this phrase, see Octavio Paz's famous essay, "The Sons of La Malinche," in *The Labyrinth of Solitude and The Other Mexico*, translated by Lysander Kemp, et al., New York: Grove Press, 1985.

And then I'm in the middle of a different America, a different American Dream. It's Friday night in Ohio, and I'm standing on the 50-yard line of a football field in the town where my mother grew up. A nuclear power plant stands no more than 1,000 yards away from the north end zone, where my great-grandfather Frank Torch lived and died in 1968. I'm standing on the 50-yard line with my grandfather, son of an Italian immigrant, and he wanted me to stand with him. The crowd is staring at us.

A few months after my mother recovered from her heart attack and brush with death, she called me up and asked me to come to Cleveland to see my Grandpa Carl get an award. "Come and surprise him, Rafa. He'd love it. The two of you always talked about football."

She paused. I knew what was coming next. She could tell I wasn't biting.

"He could die, you know."

So here we are at the 50-yard line—my mother, my uncle, my grandfather and me, along with the memory of my father and a murdered student with the same surname as me somewhere a faint dream away, a pressing matter on some part of my brain. The band plays on. They're all marching in time. There they go in their silly hats and wool suits on this fine autumn Friday night. There they go high-stepping, a majorette thrusting a baton into the air, the steel catching the light and sparkling in the night— there they go into the final hum of the national anthem.

We stand close together, the reactors smoking in the north end zone. We mouth the words. We take part. There's a game to be played.

Something always pulls me back here, driving down these familiar Chicago streets. When I came here as a boy, I was like a stranger, like my father had been for a long while and maybe still was.

And now I'm re-enacting the past but charging ahead into the future. Me, washed out, scrubbed clean. No longer Mexican, and conversely, not altogether white.

At 31 years old, fatherless again, I wonder if it was all worth it, coming here, working here. Riding along the narrow streets and broad avenues, I get the sense that I'm always coming back, like my father, pulled to the immigrant neighborhood where we started our lives. There's something about this place that fuels me. And on nights like this—the memory of the dead kid and my father hit me square in the face, battering me and throttling me forward into a time and place I do not know—riding down a street I thought I might know, I sense possibility. I sense a great awakening, a new consciousness. I come to deeper truths here in this neighborhood where fear grips me and those closest to me. There's the urgency of American lives, new ones and stagnant ones, ones to believe in.

The wasted, neon lights of 18th Street flash by the windshield. Slick, wasted boys at the street corner, angels in their regalia. Their eyes meet mine, and after a brief second there's something like recognition and then again I'm just passing through, a tourist, a *güero*. A white boy. I creep through the full simulacra of my immigrant Chicago. It sits heavy and ready to pop as a warm summer breeze comes out of nowhere and makes me want to roll down the window for a moment and take it all in again for the first time, innocent and less cynical about the future. But I don't. I charge forward, the firstborn son of a Mexican immigrant named Rafael Garcia, going slightly over the speed limit. I lock my doors, me, the Garcia boy, taking extra measures to protect myself from that which is inherently mine, all this blue-collar, immigrant urgency the street has awakened in me. Score one for cynicism and disbelief and the white boy in me.

I turn the station on the radio. There is Spanish music at the far end of the dial, and American music the farther you go up.

EPILOGUE

JUNE 17, 2011

My mother told me this morning that I should write something about how my affliction with cancer is really an affliction the whole family has in some way. I believe her. I believe it.

She says, "You should write that because we're all affected. Maybe I'll try my hand at it. Maybe I'll do it." She laughed because I don't think she even believed she would try to write it, and if she did she wouldn't show it to me. I don't need the story written by my mom; I know it's true. She's taken to itching her arms for worry over me. She's taken to a barrage of daily questions about my health and whether or not I'm following doctors' orders. She's taken to saying, "This is the one. This is the treatment." Even if I tell her not to say this, rather harshly at times because of my own superstitions, she still says it. She's always been a beacon of hope. But, being my mother, she's afflicted. She might not have what I have. But she's got the thing. We all got it.

I told her, "Do it. I don't doubt it. Write it." It's true; I don't doubt that everyone closest to me, from my best of friends to my closest of colleagues to my furthest acquaintances, is "sick," and in some way they've all been made to feel the bizarre suffering I've had to endure, but no one as much as my wife, Emily, as she is closest to me every day. She wakes to it and she's also carrying our baby, due in one month. We will keep it from him as long as possible, but no doubt, he'll be caught up in the mix. You can imagine the stupid guilt I have in all this. What stupid guilt, I know. Throw it away, people tell me.

I met my wife, Emily, about three years ago this past April. I met her online only a few months after my first round with cancer, six months after the doctors told me I had four months to live. They told me that one night, October 5, 2007, in Houston, at MD Anderson Cancer Center. Dr. Robert Benjamin gave me the news after my mom and I waited in a cramped room populated by cotton balls, heart rate monitors, various kinds of scopes and medical machinery of noises. We must have waited in that room for four hours at the very least, but it all depends on who you talk to. The more time passed, the more likely, now that I think about it, my fate was sealed. He must have been trying to clear the floor of other patients so that he could give me all the time in the world to ask questions, even if questions were the last thing on my mind. Unless he could answer for me what it meant, this turn of phrase "four months to live." Unless he could answer for me what it meant to "get one's life in order." Unless he could answer for me, "Where do we go when we die?" Unless he could excuse for me the feeling I had that I had done very little with my life and nothing really to show for it—but who does at 31?

I wanted him to be God. But he couldn't be. He was just an oncologist, and with the news he brought me, all the way from God knows where, we thought he was some kind of evil thing. He was bald and short and his lips were wet and red and saliva bunched up white and stringy at the corners of his mouth when he talked. He seemed to be wearing a perpetual frown. He was very white and it looked like he was wearing powder or some sort of base makeup. I don't know what you call it. He also wore a white doctor's jacket that went all the way down to his feet; the jacket was covered with various kinds of flair, buttons that said things like "F@#! Cancer" or "Live Each Day Like It's The Last" or "Glory in Today" or "Cancer Sucks." They were all over his jacket. It was like a big joke he was playing on me given the news he just handed me. He definitely was out of this world.

I remember saying, "What? What? What does this mean?" I remember saying it over and over again. Then I remember gagging like I was going to throw up.

My mom had great concern. She didn't cry, though. I remember that. That night, she was the strongest I've ever seen her in my entire life. It was like she was waiting her whole life for that moment. She would argue with me now having written that and shared it with you, like it was a terrible fate to be waiting for a doctor to tell her only son that he has cancer and may not survive, but my mom's reaction was so steady and so sturdy that it was like she knew it in her heart, could feel the cancer in me and knew it was in her by then. She was like a commanding officer at war with men, staring at me hard like she was telling me somehow that I'd have to be strong now. Like I'd not known what strong was and she was going to teach me. "We're going to beat this, Rafa." She kept saying it. It was a mantra, a code. She knew it her whole life. She was ready for war. Staring, leaning into the bed. "We're going to walk out of here and beat this thing, Rafa." She may have even called me "Rafael," which she never does unless I'm in trouble or she wants to tell me something important. It may have been, "Rafael. Listen to me. Rafael, we're going to get through this. You're going to win." She kept saying it. She knew this was going to happen. If she didn't, she hid it well.

(Oh, this makes me want to weep writing this. Oh, boy, makes me want to just lie down and die, the fury of a mother, the sadness, the knowing that must happen, have to happen— this feeling budding in me as I await the birth of my first child with Emily.)

Dr. Benjamin's nurse was frowning. It was very late. She looked tired, but she was taking notes. Dr. Benjamin turned to my mother when she said those things to me, and he told her she couldn't speak to me in such a way anymore, that the words we used and the language we employed now for the coming fight had to change. I thought my mom was going to kill him. I think I would have tried to kill him if it was my son sitting where I was and some doctor told me I couldn't tell my son he had to have hope. Yes, I would've, in all my rage, I would've tried to kill the doctor. My mom somehow kept her cool.

At that moment, I had the very distinct feeling of being in a Camus novel. I'd taught him enough and taught Sartre too, but it wasn't until the doctor said "four months" that I really understood the feeling of being faced with my own mortality. I would wax on for hours with my high school students, but I knew nothing. Looking back, it's funny how little I knew about anything. It's funny how little we know about anything anywhere. How much we talk. It's funny, all the jibber-jabber, the excited, racy, vapid nothing talk of the world.

It was after 9 p.m. on October 5, 2007. The night was thick with darkness. Stars here and there, but you could hardly see them because all of Houston was lit up in the distance wherever you looked. Like wildness. Like terrible hanging sadness, the yellow lights of Houston, I remember.

(Everyone had cancer. Everyone's got it. My mom's right. So, here you go, Mom.)

Where were we? What were we doing? What roads had we taken to get here?

Later, back at the hotel, my mom, like a good Italian mother, made me eat food. I remember eating bruschetta. Wolfing it down like it was the last thing I would ever eat. I remember laughing at dinner, cracking jokes and being snide, making vulgar asides that revealed a great anger that I think had always been in me, but now had been made real, brought out center stage by cancer's minions—fear and sadness. It was all so off-kilter. Like we were a boat askance in the middle of the Atlantic. Something adrift.

Miraculously, after two rounds of chemo, I had a surgery that took my cancer away for almost two years. That was in December 2007. By the end of February 2008 I found out that the woman I was married to at the time had been cheating, even before the cancer. So, I left her. In the end, after all the terror of those early months with cancer, it was like my ship had been righted. Like, the only way for me to get on with my life was to get cancer. To keep getting cancer, a constant reminder of Life. A terrible way to go, yes, a terrible row for my whole family, but, nonetheless, a lesson—a necessary season.

I had a renewed lease on life. Things were sunny. Life was good.

I met Emily a couple of months later on eharmony. When we met I was still sort of recuperating, but I had begun the long process of putting my body back together after such sickness. I met her at the Green Zebra Restaurant on the Near West Side of Chicago on April 24, 2008. I remember waiting by the bar for her and being nervous because she was very beautiful from what I could gather from the photos she had put online. I didn't know yet how tall she was, but she was blond and breathless and, from our brief correspondence, a woman who had traveled well (been to Africa, alone, to build homes with Habitat for Humanity) and wanted to see more of the world.

When she walked in, I was drinking a tonic water or something ridiculous and she asked a man who worked there about me. I don't know what she said, but by then things, as I remember them now, went into slow motion. She was talking to him, and, as it always goes with men trying to put the moves on her, the man working there said something slick to her and she laughed a little out of politeness, but she was already ignoring him and looking over the whole joint and I was standing there in the wide open. I had put some photos online, but I was embarrassed by them because they were all fairly recent and I was still bald from the chemotherapy and still sort of skinny and I remember thinking, "Why don't I have any other photos?" It was like I had come out of nowhere. "Where was the old me?" I asked my iPhoto program. I had come out of nowhere, and I thought, standing there watching her look for me, she's looking for a man from nowhere. I know it sounds strange, but I felt my stomach turn as I watched her look for me while the little man in the restaurant made slick comments or something and she towered over the place.

The man was still talking to her and she finally saw me standing by the bar. I let her look and look, and I might have let her look on and on if I could just look at her like that forever. "Oh, boy," is what I thought. "Oh, man," is what I said to myself. I may have even said it out loud, shifting the weight from one leg to the other. That's what I felt like at that time. I don't know if I fell in love with her then—it might have been some point right after—but it began there. But I think I did fall in love with her then. But I'm always so wary of such things. But no matter anymore. I fall in love with her again every time I see her in the morning. It's just the way it is. It's just the way the world works.

This great world sometimes freakishly brutal but sometimes brutishly simple and good.

When she saw me, she smiled. And I'll never forget it. A sort of relief in her face and she nodded in my direction and walked toward me with her long legs and long stride, and she was clutching her black bag, maybe out of nervousness, I don't know, but it was so lovely. She was walking up the short ramp to the bar to meet me. She was wearing a knit black shirt that hung loosely over her shoulders and it would be a lie to say that I didn't notice how beautiful her neck was and how wonderful it was to see her earrings move breathlessly across, almost tickling, the tops of her shoulders. She kept pushing her hair back behind her ears. Her mouth, a kind of sadness there, but that smile like breathless sunsets that seem to hang right there on the horizon forever, sunsets I used to experience living in Los Angeles when I was much too young to understand that somewhere later in my life I'd see the same thing in the smile of a woman I'd fall madly in love with, that I was really looking into Emily's smile. It all moved in such slow motion. I may have fallen in love with her then. I don't know. It sure sounds like it, huh?

As she nodded, I gave her some little ridiculous wave of the hand. It was stupid. She laughed a little, and when we met, she put out her hand and told me her name was Emily. I told her my name and we stood there shaking hands in a slight silence while I gathered myself because it was like I was just coming out of some long dream that I'd been in for my whole life, like being anesthetized for 32 years. I didn't know she'd be my wife then. We didn't know any of what was to come then, but we stood in the awkward silence before the maître d' came by and sat us down. I moved nervously from foot to foot like I was shadowboxing and she kept doing the thing with her hair, pushing it behind her ears and pulling her bag up on her shoulder. I don't think we ever experienced that kind of silence again. That night I told her about cancer and my past as an alcoholic, which I rarely did, and she told me about her dad, who had killed himself a couple of years earlier. At one point in the story, she said, "I don't even know why I'm telling you about this. I don't tell anyone."

I shrugged. She went on.

We closed the restaurant that night. And we closed many restaurants down other nights, too. By Thanksgiving she was my fiancée. By June she was my wife. The following month we were living in Las Vegas, trying our hand out West, following some kind of American Dream but wide awake to the potential failure of it, realizing our lives were in Chicago.

The month after we moved to Las Vegas, August, we found out my cancer had recurred. And here we are. Five recurrences later. Surgeries, chemotherapies, and now, experimental treatments by the United States government.

I've hit the big time.

Thank God for cancer. Some days, I thank God for this disease that seems to take so much from me physically, but has given so much to my heart that it makes me want to just lie down and cry about how beautiful the world is, how the road we think we're on maybe isn't the road at all, how stupid we could be on these roads we think are the right roads even when all the signs are saying "Road Closed," how hard-hearted we can be, how stubborn we are even when the signs are saying "Detour," and we keep heading down the road, even if it's saying "No Outlet." But there we go. If it wasn't for cancer I'd have already driven off the road. Falling, falling, falling. Falling away into nothing. I was that close. Put your index finger out in front of your face and put an inch between it and your thumb and that's how close I was to nothing.

When I was just a little boy, my mom would tuck me in at night before bed and I remember asking her if she loved me. She would laugh very hard and I could sense a sort of pain in her heart, like the question suggested I thought maybe she did not love me even a little. My mom would lean in close, and I remember the way she smelled in the dark, a perfume I've now long since forgotten, maybe something called "Poison" that she bought at Saks, but it doesn't matter. I remember her leaning in and bringing the covers up tight to make me feel warm and safe, and she'd tell me that she loved me like all the stars in the sky. She used to say very quietly, framed by the yellow light coming in from the bathroom of our little apartment in Mayfield Heights, Ohio, so much so that I couldn't always make out her face in the dark, "I love you more than anything, Rafael. Like every star, big and little, in the whole universe. Do you know how much that is? Do you know how many little stars there are? Do you know how many big stars there are?"

And I'd smile and I'd put my hands and arms out as far as I could stretch them and she'd laugh and say, "Yes, honey, that's it. And you don't forget it. That's how much I love you."

When she'd go away and close the door a little, enough for some of the light to come in my room, a certain slant of light, I remember trying to think about her brand of infinity. I'd stare out the window or hard into the wall of my room and let my gaze go slack trying to see the universe in such a way, such infinite love.

Now, I have the distinct knowledge of how far away I am from nothing. Little did my mom know that when she was telling me that when I was such a young boy that she was really telling me how far I was from nothing, how far we all are if we just pay attention to the dumb thing we're in called Life.

So, yes, my mom's right. We all have cancer. But the cancer I got, the cancer I'm talking about, let it grow, let it metastasize. Let it grow all over us as a family. Let it grow, father. Let it come, mother. Let it feed, wife, and let it grow and eat, friends, and let it grow fat, child. So shall I. So shall I. It'll be enough love to eat for a hundred thousand years of suffering. A million trillion. Arms wide open.

AFTERWORD

by EMILY OLSON-TORCH

The night Rafael died, I crawled into bed next to him. There had been a house full of friends and family just hours before, but now all was quiet. His last visitor, perhaps his closest friend, had flown in from California, and just left. Rafael hadn't been conscious since earlier in the morning. There, but not there. Our queen-size bed had been replaced with a hospital bed; a necessity lurking large in our small bedroom. My head was on his chest and I could hear the beat of his heart. It was as if I had been summoned; somehow knowing it was the end.

Three months prior, Rafael and I had found out his fate with cancer had been sealed. The conclusion we had long considered, but desperately worked against, was now inevitable. Rafael was the one who decided how he wanted to handle what he called the noble act of dying. As he explained it, the way you die is just as important as the way you live. Rafael, determined and motivated until the bitter end, went about the important business of getting his life in order.

Rafael wanted to die at home, so we hunkered down in our condo, an old factory space, maybe 1,000 square feet. Our baby, Rocco, was asleep in a crib just outside of our bedroom. He was just 4 months old.

I'm not sure how long I stayed there like that, with my head on Rafael's chest. But as I lay with him, scared of the separate paths we were about to take, I listened to the beat of his heart and tried to match my breath with his as if willing a way for us to become one again. Over time, as his breath grew shallower, his heartbeat became softer and slower. He was right there but we were falling farther and farther away from one another. I lifted my head to whisper in his ear, "I'll see you again; it will just seem like a minute." I repeated it over and over. When I lay back down on his chest, his heart had stopped beating.

Rafael had faced cancer once before me. When we met, he was working through the intensity of being so close to death, only to be snatched away from the edge and saved. But saved for how long? Would the cancer come back? When would the cancer come back?

Part of our living, the building of our life together, was to confront this cancerous beast that was stalking Rafael. To love each other fully, we had to learn how to balance the real possibility of death with the overwhelming desire for us to have the life we so desperately wanted. So together we worked through what death was. What it meant.

Rafael taught me that learning how to live is about learning how to die. Dying happens with certainty to all of us. At first glance, there is a darkness around death, but Rafael, a skeptic at first, worked hard and challenged himself to move away from the darkness and ultimately find that death, like life, is full of wonder and awe and light. We had moved away from death and found hope.

We found and held hope even as the cancer recurred and then recurred and then recurred. I suppose it's crazy to have a child when you're potentially dying of cancer, but despite all the treatments and surgeries, we really wanted to have a baby. Rafael was adamant that we try in vitro fertilization. Our hope carried us as we balanced my blood tests with his chemo treatments. No matter the toll cancer surgeries and treatments made on his body, there was something very strong and steady about Rafael. I believed in him. He wasn't scared.

A few weeks after Rocco was born, we found out Rafael was terminal. It was then that we started our long goodbye. We talked and talked. And he continued to write, all the way up until the end. He had always written as a way to understand people, to understand the world, and now, I think, to try to make sense of his life. *The Garcia Boy*, the great work of his life, was his constant companion for many years. He would add and subtract, revise and edit as the years rolled past. He was on a perpetual journey to seek out a deeper understanding of life circumstances, and he documented what he witnessed and learned in his writing. He would gravitate to different parts of the text, taking what he needed from his family story in order to better understand himself. Drafts of this book were shaped by Rafael's reflection and wisdom over the years. While he never felt he got it just right, this text brought him acceptance and peace.

At the end, Rafael and his biological father weren't on speaking terms. During the time I knew Rafael, he was in contact with his biological father only once. It was early on in our relationship and all I can think now is that it must have been some sort of final meeting. To me, Rafael was putting that chapter of his life behind him. Soon after this meeting, Rafael confided in me that he wanted Tom, his stepfather, to legally adopt him. At the time I recall being surprised by such a symbolic act, especially by a grown man. In hindsight I can see this for what it was. Rafael was reflecting on his life as if it were a narrative and this was one area he could rewrite, revise to apply the right meaning in the right place to the right person. Tom was a guiding light for Rafael, sturdy and strong, especially during the years of his sobriety. Rafael had found a means of rewriting his own history in a way that bound him to the man he viewed as his father.

Rafael left me with many gifts, but probably the most selfless gift was his blessing that my life was to go on after he was gone. He made it clear to me, and to my circle of closest family and friends, that I was to find love. I was to be happy. Even if it meant forgetting about him, I was to do this. Above all, he told me that I couldn't let his death make me hard.

Looking back now, our time together feels sort of like a distant dream. Immediately following his death, I was thrust into my new life. I was learning to be a mother, immersing myself in work and navigating my new daily routines. That first year was probably the most difficult as I celebrated all the beautiful joys of Rocco's firsts — Christmas, holidays, birthday — with the overwhelming grief of each milestone being the first without Rafael.

As time has worn on, so has my relationship with grief. Slowly I've been able to start remembering Rafael again, making space to allow those memories to come to the surface, and sharing those with Rocco. It was during this time that I first heard from Miles Harvey about the opportunity to partner with

Big Shoulders Books to publish *The Garcia Boy*. I had some reservations at first. As selfish as it may sound, I wasn't sure if I was ready to share Rafael's story yet. For all the talking we did before his death, one thing that went unsaid was what to do with his writing. He had methodically organized all his files, countless drafts, letters and revisions, leaving everything in good order. I think he knew that once I was ready I would seek this out as a way to remember him. And it was. It's through his writing that he can still offer me some sort of reassurance, a comfort— proof that my reality had actually been real. That I wasn't making this up or waking from a dream. Turning to his writing wasn't the same as having him here with us, but it was the part of him that Rocco and I had now.

Miles was politely persistent about the project, and I accepted a meeting with him. Miles had an almost contagious enthusiasm for the Big Shoulders program and it was clear Rafael's work had left an impression on him. Within the first few minutes of our meeting, I knew this was the perfect match. The idea of collaborating with students, debating points in the text, reminded me of dinner conversations Rafael and I used to have when he would recount his day as a high school teacher. Yes, I remember thinking to myself, this is how to get this book published.

For countless reasons, it's tough being the one left behind after losing a spouse. There's pressure in being the storyteller, the memory holder, because you are the half of the whole who gets to live. You become your own relentless critic of your ability and worthiness to carry on in a good enough way. I've struggled with this pressure as I work with the editing team from Big Shoulders Books. I've had to make many decisions about what to leave in and what to take out of a story that isn't mine; that doesn't belong to me. Somehow, through this process I've had to learn to be okay with that. Bringing this book to life allows Rafael to once again have a voice. And I no longer need to bear the burden of being the only storyteller for Rocco. Words can't describe my gratitude to Miles and all the students who have allowed me the privilege of sharing Rafael's work with the world.

AUTHOR'S
ACKNOWLEDGMENTS

The Garcia Boy would not have been possible without the generous support, love and feedback of the following people, in no particular order: my mother and father, Tari and Tom; Caitlin Sweeney; Ross Thomas; Eric Martinez; Carolyn Alessio; Jean Gregorek; Anne Bohlen; Cyndy Olson; Aunt Lee; Lee and Cathy Clasper-Torch; Chris Torch; Adam O'Neil; Kyle Banker; the late Joseph Nemeth; Leon and Amy Kass; the family of Kyler Yelverton (in memory of him); Steven Cavallero; Freddie Ward; Dana Larson; and Jeremy Gregerson. And thank you to my students, both past and present—what with all their thesis statements and topic sentences and textual evidence. Oh, the things you've given me, a lifetime of wonder and gratitude. Yes! to my students.

And, of course, this book is nothing without the intensity and passion of my wildly intelligent and beautiful wife, Emily Olson-Torch. I tell her that I loved her right when she walked in the door of that restaurant on our first date, and she says that it isn't possible that I loved her right away because we hadn't said anything to each other yet.

And I tell her, Yes. Yes, it is possible.

—RAFAEL TORCH

EDITOR'S
ACKNOWLEDGMENTS

Because Big Shoulders Books is a collaborative enterprise, many people have played crucial roles in the making of this book. I would like to thank the following:

•   Rafael Torch, for living a meaningful life and for observing it with such perceptiveness and passion. Those of us who worked on *The Garcia Boy* count ourselves among his many grateful students.

•   Emily Olson-Torch, for her trust, her open-mindedness, her gift for collaboration, her beautifully written afterword and her inspiring devotion to Rafael and his work. No writer could have a better champion.

•   The gifted student editors from DePaul's graduate and undergraduate creative-writing programs, for all their hard work, all their productive disagreements, all their innovations in shaping this manuscript and all their lessons for a certain middle-aged professor.

•   Associate managing editors Travis Murphy and Matthew J. Postlewaite, and managing editors Kaitlin Lounsberry and Brittany Schmitt, for their countless hours and their endless insights. They did flat-out wonderful work.

•   Achy Obejas, for helping to get this project off the ground and for her dazzling foreword.

•   Two great professionals — designer Natalie Mills Bontumasi and copy editor Becky Maughan — for lending their talent and expertise to this project.

+ Gifted publicist Sheryl Johnston, for teaching the Big Shoulders Books promotion course for *The Garcia Boy* and for astute input on this project, as well as on *How Long Will I Cry?: Voices of Youth Violence*, a book that owes much of its success to her.

+ The faculty and staff at Cristo Rey Jesuit High School, for their encouragement and generosity of spirit, as well as for their great work with young people. Special thanks to Antonio Ortiz, Bernhard Walke and Jennifer Sirota, as well as to former Cristo Rey teacher Lauren Gatti.

+ Carolyn Alessio, for her guidance, sensitivity and outreach efforts. I am deeply grateful to this busy writer and teacher for interrupting her schedule to go the extra mile for Rafael and his former students.

+ Other generous individuals who have provided input and support: José Miguel Acosta-Córdova, Eric Canan, Cathy Clark, Mary Devona Stark, Meredith Ferrill, Janet Hickey, Eric Houghton, Rebecca Johns-Trissler, Bill Johnson González, Sara Miller-Acosta, Jeremy Mulderig, Francesca Royster, Tari Torch-Sweeney, Tom Sweeney, Jon Tribble and Christopher Watkins.

+ The Illinois Arts Council, which long ago provided Rafael Torch with both a Fellowship for Prose and a Literary Arts Award grant. This book is proof that such investments in promising writing careers are essential, even when the payoff takes years.

+ Michele Morano and Chris Green, my fellow founding editors at Big Shoulders Books, for dreaming big, and David Welch, BSB managing editor, for making big dreams happen.

+ Irene and William Beck for their generosity, friendship, counsel and collaboration. Without them, Big Shoulders Books would never have been possible, and this book would simply not exist.

—MILES HARVEY

ABOUT OUR BOOKS

If you liked *The Garcia Boy*, please consider ordering one of the other extraordinary titles from Big Shoulders Books.

WRITE YOUR HEART OUT

If you are, or have ever been, a teen or interested in relationships or inspired to write by something you've read, this is the book for you. By turns moving, funny, sweet and painful, the 44 personal stories of *Write Your Heart Out* capture teen life as it really is. From crushes to heartbreak to the complexities of family love, teen writers offer insights into how we learn to negotiate relationships and what it means to reflect on experience. *Write Your Heart Out* includes writing prompts and blank pages, so grab a pen and get ready to tell your own stories!

I REMEMBER

I Remember: Chicago Veterans of War weaves together the memories of 50 veterans of World War II, Korea, Vietnam, Bosnia, Iraq and Afghanistan. Using "I remember" statements that capture the small and large details of firsthand experience, this book illustrates both the constant and ever-changing nature of war and its aftermath.

HOW LONG WILL I CRY?

In 2011 and 2012, while more than 900
people were being murdered on the streets
of Chicago, creative-writing students
from DePaul University fanned out across
the city to interview people whose lives have
been changed by the bloodshed. The result
is *How Long Will I Cry?: Voices of Youth
Violence*, an extraordinary and eye-opening
oral history. Told by real people in their own
words, the stories in this book are harrowing, heartbreaking
and full of hope.

HOW TO ORDER

Our books are FREE. The editors ask that by taking a copy,
you agree to donate money or time to a group working to make
Chicago or your own community a better place. We also ask
that you tell us a story about why you want the book.

To order copies or learn more: **bigshouldersbooks.com**

The editors welcome requests from teachers, community
activists, librarians and members of the clergy. We reserve
the right to refuse requests that we find inappropriate
or impractical.

ABOUT THE EDITORIAL TEAM

CHRIS GREEN (BSB founding editor) is the author of *The Sky Over Walgreens, Epiphany School* and *Résumé*. His poetry has appeared in such publications as *Poetry, The New York Times, New Letters* and *Nimrod*. He has edited four anthologies, including *I Remember: Chicago Veterans of War*. He teaches in the English department at DePaul University. More information can be found at www.chrisgreenpoetry.com.

MILES HARVEY (editor of *The Garcia Boy* and BSB founding editor) is the editor of *How Long Will I Cry?: Voices of Youth Violence*, a collection of oral histories now in its sixth edition with more than 40,000 copies in circulation. His other books include *The Island of Lost Maps: A True Story of Cartographic Crime* and *The King of Confidence* (forthcoming from Little, Brown & Company). He is an associate professor of English at DePaul University.

SHERYL JOHNSTON (book publicity professor) is a longtime publicist, writer and event producer. Between 1998 and 2015, she co-produced and publicized the annual Story Week Festival of Writers presented by the Columbia College Chicago fiction writing department. Earlier in her career, she was an editorial writer at WLS-TV, a vice president at J. Walter Thompson USA and president of her own PR agency. She is currently a literary publicist for authors throughout the country.

BECKY MAUGHAN (copy editor) has been an editor in Chicago for over 20 years. She has worked in marketing, advertising and journalism.

NATALIE MILLS BONTUMASI (book designer) has been a graphic designer in Chicago for over 20 years. Her company, Good Thomas Design, focuses on nonprofit organizations and small businesses. Her work is included in the Chicago Design Archive.

MICHELE MORANO (BSB founding editor) is the author of *Grammar Lessons: Translating a Life in Spain* and many published essays and stories. She is a creative-writing professor and chair of the English department at DePaul University.

ACHY OBEJAS (foreword) is the author of *The Tower of the Antilles*, which was nominated for a PEN/Faulkner award. Her other books include *Ruins* and *Days of Awe*. As a translator, she's worked with Wendy Guerra, Rita Indiana, Junot Díaz and Megan Maxwell, among others. A native of Havana, she currently lives in the San Francisco Bay area.

EMILY OLSON-TORCH (afterword) is the vice president of e-commerce and marketing at Honey-Can-Do, a multinational manufacturer of home storage and organization products. This job gives her the opportunity to work with student interns from Chicago's Cristo Rey Jesuit High School, where her late husband taught.

DAVID WELCH (BSB managing editor) is the author of *Everyone Who Is Dead* (Spork Press) and *It Is Such a Good Thing to Be in Love With You* (GreenTower Press). He is assistant director of publishing and outreach in the English department at DePaul University, where he teaches creative writing and popular literature.

RAFAEL TORCH (1975–2011) was a prize-winning essayist whose work appeared in such publications as *Antioch Review, Indiana Review, North American Review* and *Crab Orchard Review*, the latter two of which have named literary awards in his honor. He earned his Master of Arts in the humanities from the University of Chicago, where his thesis, an early draft of *The Garcia Boy*, was the recipient of the Catherine Ham Memorial Award for Excellence in graduate work. During his teaching career, he worked at Cristo Rey Jesuit High School in Chicago, the Latin School of Chicago and The Meadows School in Las Vegas.